THE CHINA STRATEGY

THE CHINA STRATEGY

Harnessing the Power
of the World's
Fastest-Growing Economy

EDWARD TSE

BASIC
BOOKS
A Member of the Perseus Books Group
New York

Published by Basic Books,
A Member of the Perseus Books Group

Books published by Basic Books are available at special discounts for bulk purchases in the United States by corporations, institutions, and other organizations. For more information, please contact the Special Markets Department at the Perseus Books Group, 2300 Chestnut Street, Suite 200, Philadelphia, PA 19103, or call (800) 810–4145, ext. 5000, or e-mail special.markets@perseusbooks.com.

Designed by Brent Wilcox

Library of Congress Cataloging-in-Publication Data
Tse, Edward.
    The China strategy : how to win the new game of global enterprise / Edward Tse.
        p.   cm.
    Includes bibliographical references and index.
    ISBN 978-0-465-01825-3 (alk. paper)
    1. New business enterprises—China.   2. Economic development—China.
3. China—Economic policy—21st century.   4. Cities and towns—Growth.
5. Globalization—China.   I. Title.
    HD62.5.T77 2009
    330.973—dc22

                                                             2009040369

10 9 8 7 6 5 4 3 2 1

To Grace, Karen, and Kevin

CONTENTS

CHAPTER 1

The Country That Cannot Be Ignored

L I NING IS ONE of China's most instantly recognizable faces. He shot to fame in 1984, winning six medals in gymnastics competitions at the Los Angeles Olympics, three of them gold. Since then, he has remained in the spotlight by becoming one of the country's most successful businessmen as the owner of China's largest sportswear company. The eponymous Li Ning brand has more than 7,550 retail outlets across the country and annual sales of more than $980 million.

The Li Ning Company Limited is still tiny compared with Nike and Adidas, whose global revenues in 2008 were $18.6 billion and $15.9 billion respectively. But Li Ning's growth is faster; its global marketing, still in the beginning stages, includes sponsorships of major league basketball in the United States, Argentina, and Spain.[1]

Then the 2008 Olympics went to Beijing. Li Ning was chosen to light the torch at the opening ceremonies in Beijing's Bird Nest stadium, in front of a television audience of more than a billion viewers. The moment must have been particularly difficult for Adidas, which had spent a quarter of a billion dollars on Olympic sponsorships and marketing during the run-up to the games. Suddenly, here was not just one of China's most famous former Olympic gold medalists, but one of their leading business rivals—and a living symbol of the intent, ambition, and competitive spirit of Chinese enterprise. In a handful of seconds, he stole the show from his Western competitors.

China has hundreds of thousands of Li Nings: entrepreneurs who have driven one of the fastest sustained national economic growth rates of any country in world history. They may not all be as successful as Li. But after decades of being held back by their country's adoption of socialism, they and the rest of the Chinese population are moving forward with the force of water gushing from a broken dam. The intensity of their aspirations, joined with the plans of the government and the presence of the country's hundreds of millions of ordinary people, suggests that future developments in China will overshadow even the momentous changes of the recent past—and in a way that affects the strategy, and even the identity, of companies around the world.

Indications of China's new identity are everywhere. They were evident in the enormous haul of gold medals that Chinese athletes won at the 2008 Olympics. They are also evident in the stunning modern architecture of Beijing, Shanghai, and other cities; the cornucopia of products that fills the shops and stores of China's cities; in the country's Internet and mobile-phone user bases, both the largest of any nation; and in the market capitalization of Industrial and Commercial Bank of China, the world's most valuable bank. Perhaps the most significant indicator is the increasing presence of China's investment and business presence in every other major region, from Africa to Europe to the Indian subcontinent to the Americas. This wave of energy and entrepreneurship is changing the world, but its impact has just begun to be felt, and it is still often misunderstood, both by foreigners and by China's own people.

A large number of businesspeople have gained experience in China in the last decade. They believe they understand how to operate there, and they have built their business models on expectations of a relatively stable, coherent, expanding future for their Chinese operations.

But the intensity and scale of change in China means that all businesses, even those that are currently successful, will find themselves inadequately prepared for the turmoil and dynamism to come. And if they aren't prepared for the new China emerging today, their companies are likely to falter. They will not just miss out on the opportunities in this economy; they will be pushed aside by rivals, old and new, that use China to transform their competitive position.

For in the world's fastest-growing economy, the experience of the last ten years will not be the best guide to the next ten years. Business leaders around the world who want to be successful—not just in China, but anywhere—will need a new China strategy.

A new China strategy does not merely mean a set of plans for doing business in China. Most large companies are already selling to China's markets and competing against Chinese companies. Many more, even relatively small enterprises, will join them. But a true China strategy is different. It is a *one world* strategy: a long-range developmental plan for doing business as a global enterprise in which China is a central and integrated component, in a world where China plays a very different role than it has in the past.

Corporate leaders who see China as a large but still-emerging market must come to see it as a diverse and immense group of global consumers. Those who see Chinese companies as partners in joint ventures must come to see those companies as active, highly capable global competitors. And those who see the Chinese government as simultaneously welcoming and opaque must come to see it as an active, increasingly open player on the global stage. In other words, they must see this country in the same way that the corporate leaders of the late nineteenth century saw the still-emerging United States of America.

Changing this paradigm, and seeing the Chinese market and government in this new light, will not be easy. It will feel unfamiliar and challenging for many companies, even those that have operated successfully in China over the past ten years. The Chinese themselves have only just started digesting the implications of the changes they are going through. Having experienced such rapid growth, they are now looking at its impact—managing the effect on its environment and figuring out what sort of companies should be fostered and which discouraged. They are also trying to ensure that the wealth being created benefits more than the coastal rim of the nation, that workers interests are protected, and that companies and industries can move up the value chain.

As for multinational companies—or "foreign" companies, as the Chinese think of them—they still have a lot to learn about China itself. As the country matures and becomes more integrated with the outside world, more of its context becomes visible: its diverse markets and demographics, policies and regulations, cultures and tastes. Accessible as China has proved itself in the last two decades, it remains a country whose distinctive characteristics both create opportunities for businesses and constrain them.

Some companies appreciate this already. IBM's quest to become a "globally integrated enterprise," in large part through an expanded Chinese presence, is explored later in this book. But too many have yet to acquire the degree of sophistication necessary to appreciate both where potential may lie and the nature of the problems likely to be encountered in realizing it. On the plus side, most have abandoned the very worst simplicities, epitomized by the meaningless but often repeated phrase "a market of 1.3 billion." Yet there remains a widespread tendency to underestimate both the complexity that exists already and the increasingly broad range of opportunities the country offers for companies seeking to enhance their global as well as their Chinese competitiveness.

Scale and Intensity

Very few leaders in the West were prepared for the speed of economic recovery in China in 2009. Even now, few are prepared for the way in which China (along with a few other Asian nations) will provide an engine for the global economy going forward. In the first nine months of 2009, automobile sales in China rose to 9.66 million units, up 34 percent from the year before—and at a time when worldwide vehicle sales were falling. In September 2009, net profits for the top five hundred companies reached $170.6 billion, exceeding for the first time the monthly net profits ($98.9 billion) reported by the top five hundred companies in the United States.[2]

To be sure, numbers like these result in part from the enormous investment made by the Chinese government in economic stimulus after the economic crisis began; but they also reflect the fundamental growth potential of the Chinese market, the resilience and energy of its entrepreneurs, and the determination and flexibility of its government. Most important, they demonstrate how rapidly the Chinese economy continues to evolve.

Every major dimension of China will be different during the next decade than it was through most of the 2000s. New leading companies will emerge; the appetites and tastes of consumers will shift; and China's government will pursue priorities that are very different from the priorities of the reform program that Deng Xiaoping launched in 1978. Much of this change is still uncertain. Most specific predictions are unreliable, because the country is on a nonlinear trajectory that is generating enormous, discontinuous change.

But it is possible to define and track the two major forces—scale and intensity—that have given China its unique power and position today. No other country, not even India, has these two factors in such potent combination.

China's scale, of course, stems from the size of its population: with 1.3 billion people, it is larger than any other country in the world. (India has 1.1 billion.) Although it is a highly diverse population, it is also remarkably coherent for its size. The Han people make up 92 percent of China's population, and while they speak an enormous range of dialects and variations, they share a single written language and almost everyone can speak the official spoken language, Putonghua. Thus, anything that happens in China is magnified by its immense demographics, making the Chinese influential, even when they prefer to be obscure. This scale helps to explain why many international companies will continue to be active in China, no matter what else happens. Success in China, either for a local entrepreneur or a global multinational, is enough to transform a company's performance worldwide. For international firms, a Chinese presence allows them to expand their reach to one-fifth of the world's population. For domestic companies, it provides a base more than large enough to generate the scale needed for sustained success; for some, even an assault on overseas markets. Most companies will continue to be drawn to the Chinese economy, which grew at around 10 percent annually for three decades, and which may plausibly return to that rate as it continues to recover from the 2008 recession.

Within a few decades, China's economy will replace the United States' as the world's largest. Exactly when this will happen depends on a range of variables, among them exchange rate fluctuations. But regardless of the exact date, one of the safer predictions for the first half of the twenty-first century is that China's growth, supported by that of India and several other countries, will make Asia the source of more than half the world's gross domestic product by around 2030—up from less than one-fifth in 1950, and one-quarter in 1973.[3] This represents an overall shift in the center of the world's economic gravity, the likes of which has not been seen since the industrial revolution powered the West's rise to economic preeminence just over two centuries ago. Even a widespread return to trade protectionism would not derail this outcome.

China's intensity—the ferocious entrepreneurial energy and productivity emerging in every part of this country—will have even greater impact than its scale. This intensity stems in part from the deep-seated desire of the Chinese people to regain their historical primacy, taking back what they see as China's rightful place on the world stage. Even the vigor and entrepreneurial activity of India will not match that of China, at least for the next decade.

Beginning in the early 1800s, after the Qing dynasty had passed its peak, China experienced a period of technological and economic stagnation. Mao Zedong's revolution, culminating in the Communist Party's rise to power in 1949, ended a long period of civil war and foreign intervention, but the central planning that followed was an economic disaster, especially during the Cultural Revolution of 1966–1976. Although that period of extreme authoritarianism came to an end with Mao's death in 1976 and the ascension to power of Deng Xiaoping two years later, it took two more decades to clear the ground and lay the foundations for China's economic reemergence.

Only in 1992, when Deng Xiaoping made his now-famous "southern visit" to the city of Shenzhen, was the current wave of economic momentum unleashed. By then, the pressure of pent-up economic demand and ambition had been building for a long time. And it did not abate during the first few years of economic growth; it only became stronger. After growing up in a value system built on two ideas—"Life is good under communism" and the Confucian edict "Acceptable behavior is determined by the authority of the parent, boss, and leader"—Chinese businesspeople are now questioning the efficacy of those values.

Today, there is one question in the mind of every fledgling entrepreneur in the high-tech start-ups of Beijing's Zhongguancun neighborhood, the private factories of Wenzhou on the Zhejiang coast south of Shanghai, the manufacturers of Dongguan just north of Hong Kong, and dozens of other Chinese business centers: "Why not me?" These young Chinese businesspeople see the rewards of success all around them. They are driven by materialistic desires, eager to catch up with the rest of the world, and almost giddy with a sense of multiplying opportunity. They have read Internet chronicles of the triumphs of Amazon, Google, and Facebook, and in navigating the economic crisis of 2008–2009, they have become well aware of their country's economic strength. They see themselves as the creators of the world's future Intels, Apples, and Microsofts, and some of them undoubtedly will be.

Since the early 2000s, this intensity has produced the China that the world sees today. It is almost certain to continue and accelerate. Its force and volatility explains why China's future is unpredictable, and why many foreign (non-Chinese) companies may experience a bumpier ride than they expect.

A Decade of Difference

Another factor has tempered China's growth and helped to ensure its viability in the long run. The nation's economy has been thoroughly restructured during the past decades. China has achieved a level of flexibility and competitiveness far greater than it had in the mid-1990s.

The principal change in China's restructuring has been the elimination of most of its centrally planned, state-controlled economy. State-owned enterprises (SOEs) remain, but these are stripped-down versions of the dinosaurs of a decade ago. The largest and most important of them—including China Mobile, the leading mobile-communications operator, and China Petroleum & Chemical Corporation, an oil and gas giant—are tightly managed and for the most part profitable. Outside of these companies, a Chinese economy has sprung up with a large and growing number of privately owned smaller companies, supplemented by a small but disproportionately influential group of foreign-invested businesses. In this economy, prices for most goods and services are set by the market. The labor force is flexible, increasingly well educated, and continually improving its skills.

The Chinese banking system has also been reorganized and, in the process, shed all but a tiny portion of its nonperforming loans. A decade ago, China's financial infrastructure was a mess, with a technically insolvent banking sector weighed down with nonperforming loans to SOEs. By the second half of 2009, however, China had the world's largest foreign currency reserves at just over $2 trillion. It was the world's largest holder of U.S. Treasury bonds, valued at $801.5 billion in May 2009.[4] And as I noted earlier, the world's largest bank (measured by market capitalization) was the Industrial and Commercial Bank of China. Similarly, China's trading status has risen from negligible to that of a world leader: its imports and exports are the equivalent of about 60 percent of gross domestic product (GDP).[5] In the United States and Japan, they account for about 25 percent of GDP.

The liberalization of China's economy has involved an extraordinary expansion of infrastructure: airports, sea ports, power stations, mobile and fixed-line telecom networks, expressways, and railroad lines, almost all of which have been developed to world standards and beyond. Beijing's new airport, built for the Olympics, has received widespread media attention, but it is just one of countless achievements over the past decade. Among them are the world's highest-altitude railway, running 714 miles to the Tibetan capital, Lhasa, and built at a cost of $3.5 billion; the Yangshan deep-water port, constructed more than 18 miles offshore at a cost of $12.5 billion, which has made nearby Shanghai the world's busiest cargo destination; and one of the world's fastest railways, the maglev in Shanghai, with a top speed of almost 270 miles per hour.[6] This is a part of China's ambitious $300 billion cross-country high-speed railroad-building program.

China's reform era has also produced a string of glittering twenty-first-century metropolises, each with a population in the millions. Shanghai is the most famous of these, with its magnificent skyline, ultrachic restaurants and nightlife, and a population of more than 14 million people. Surrounding it in the Yangtze River Delta are a host of other rapidly developing urban centers, including Suzhou, Hangzhou, Nanjing, Ningbo, and Wuxi, each with its own unique history. Together, they are home to burgeoning electronics, chemical, semiconductor, automotive, and software industries.

In the south, the Pearl River Delta in the Guangdong province produces about 30 percent of China's total exports. Also in this province, on the border with Hong Kong, is Shenzhen, China's biggest boom-town, with a population that has grown from less than 100,000 in 1979 to more than 10 million today. In the northeast is Dalian, which has long been favored by Japanese corporations. Tianjin, a port city just sixty-eight miles of expressway from Beijing and the leading industrial center in northern China, is home to Motorola's multibillion-dollar mobile-phone operation and one of Toyota's two principal China plants and is a focal area of development by the Chinese central government. A little farther down the coast lies Qingdao, famous for its beer, but also home to northern China's busiest port. Like all the other cities of the Shandong peninsula, it is very popular with South Korean companies. Below Shanghai are the provinces of Zhejiang, the heartland of privately owned business in China and home to legions of the country's entrepreneurs, and Fujian, opposite Taiwan, whose growth will inevitably surge now that there are direct transportation links between the island and China's mainland.

Along the length of China's 11,000 miles of coastline, the story is the same—cities with highly dynamic economies, home to the vast majority of China's middle class, packed with goods to buy, and host to tens of thousands of new companies, most of them privately owned. Most of these cities have new airports; they are all linked to each other via expressways, and are governed by officials who are eager to attract as much new business as they can.

The driver of all this growth has been the interrelationship and interplay between China's market liberalization and its positioning as a key part of the global value chain for an ever greater number of companies. Hence one core theme of this book: to flourish over the next decade and beyond, multinational companies must formulate strategies that can integrate the business implications of China's market liberalization into their global value chains. And if they hope to succeed in this, they must understand not just the China of the past twenty years, but also the forces that will change this country as it moves forward.

A Very New and Old Nation

The scale and intensity of the Chinese economy was not diminished by the global economic crisis of 2008 to any long-lasting extent. At first, the manufacturing sector was hurt badly by the decline in demand for China's exports, particularly from the developed world. And like the United States, China recovered in part through a massive government stimulus—almost $600 billion, announced in November 2008 and put into play rapidly. But unlike the United States, where the recession marked the end of an era of growth built on unsustainable practices (especially in the financial sector), the downturn caused only a temporary hiatus in China's growth; annualized growth shrank to 2 percent in the winter but was heading back toward 8 percent by July. By October, the Chinese recovery was generally recognized as under way; overall GDP growth for the year was expected to be between 7 and 8 percent.[7]

Moreover, the recession enhanced the position of Chinese companies and their relationships with overseas enterprises. By September, Wang Jiming, the vice president of the Chinese Enterprise Confederation (the preeminent Chinese association of business leaders), was able to say that Chinese companies were not as vulnerable to the crisis as their American counterparts.[8]

The reason for this robustness had to do with fundamentals. China had rid itself of most of the structural rigidities inherited from socialism, its national productivity was rising, and its economy was beginning to develop its own consumer base.

The stimulus itself was deliberately designed to improve these fundamentals: as *New Republic* writer Zachary Karabell put it, "Within a few months, money was being put to work—primarily on infrastructure projects in the interior of the country, but also on . . . measures such as handing out pre-paid cards to encourage consumer spending . . . The central government also mandated . . . a more open approach to lending . . . The stimulus accelerated the long-term goal of the Beijing government to focus more on internal demand and interior development and less on export-driven activity."[9]

In retrospect, the primary cause of slowing economic growth within China can in large part be attributed to the overheated nature of its own real estate and construction sectors. As property prices fell sharply through 2008, demand from the construction industry for steel, cement, and other industrial products dropped sharply, and the government responded with an investment-driven stimulus package. In effect, China slowed down to take a breath and shed some of the extra capacity that built up during a run of unprecedented growth stretching from the late 1990s to early 2008. The economic slowdown may have helped accelerate this process by stimulating a much-needed round of consolidation across many of the country's industries.

The next five to ten years will see the emergence of a new generation of Chinese companies, bigger but leaner, better able to compete, and prepared to operate on a global basis. Over the next five years, while American automakers are still fixing their problems at home, some of China's car companies will expand overseas. Similarly, while American and European banks are sorting out the consequences of a financial morass of their own making, some of China's leading financial institutions will plan growth strategies built on international expansion. And while American and European telecommunications equipment makers are downsizing and restructuring, their Chinese competitors will be claiming a larger share of international markets.

Of course, not every Chinese company will thrive, but many are in strong positions to take advantage of the recession. For instance, they will exploit major declines in corporate valuations in Europe and North America to buy companies headquartered on those continents. Outbound investment by Chinese companies has been rising rapidly— from around $5 billion in 2004 to $27 billion in 2007, then almost doubling to $52 billion in 2008.[10]

It is easy to overstate the extent to which the Chinese people feel they are sharing a national mission, especially in the aftermath of an economic crisis. But it is no exaggeration to say that for the majority of Chinese, national identity is an important factor in determining their actions and in their acquiescence to their country's political system. After falling steadily and further behind the West during the nineteenth and twentieth centuries and having endured so much internecine conflict, the country is rediscovering a sense of national pride. The Chinese reaction to the Olympics and the importance attached to hosting the games makes this very clear.

The Chinese also display a striking amount of openness in their current national character: manifest, for example, in their willingness to embrace new ideas and technologies. This is easier to understand when you consider that since the early twentieth century, the Chinese people have weathered relentless upheaval. As recently as the mid-1990s, the closure of tens of thousands of state-owned enterprises led to the layoffs of tens of millions of workers. The growth of China's export manufacturing sector led to the migration of more than a hundred million country dwellers from the poor central and inland regions to the coastal manufacturing centers. The Chinese learned that they could take this change in stride and life would improve.

As a consequence, the closed attitude of the isolated Celestial Empire that the West confronted two centuries ago is evolving into a national mindset that wants to mix with the outside world, and expects that outsiders will recognize their achievements. That's why hosting the Olympics was so symbolically important.

There is a historical precedent for this evolving worldview. It was prominent in China during the Tang Dynasty, which spanned nearly three hundred years from the seventh to tenth centuries. That, too, was a time of great commerce and cosmopolitan openness. It was the golden era of the Silk Road, China's link to central Asia, the Middle East, and Europe. Maritime trade flourished, with Chinese ships sailing as far as the Persian Gulf, Red Sea, and Africa. Trade with Japan and Korea was extensive, and Arab and Persian merchants established outposts in China, especially in Guangzhou. Thousands of foreigners lived in the country, and its capital, Chang'an (now Xi'an), was the world's largest city. There was a vibrant mix of religious and philosophical ideas; Buddhism flourished alongside Taoism and Confucianism. Culture flourished, too; this was the period of China's greatest poets. There was also an explosion of technology and innovation, with woodblock printing contributing to the advancement of medicine, geography, cartography, mechanics, horology, and engineering.

The current era is also one of openness to new ideas. China's economic reforms since 1990 have been launched with a strong focus on technological innovation. One of the core goals has been the acquisition of technology and expertise, and the results can be seen in everything from China's space and nuclear power programs to its telecommunications and computing prowess. This effort also laid the foundations for a whole series of "pillar" industries (as the most fundamental business-enabling sectors are called in China), including automobiles, telecommunications equipment, electronics, semiconductors, nuclear power, aerospace, and specialty chemicals. And the government continues to emphasize the need to gain the skills and know-how that will be required to prosper as the global economy becomes more and more knowledge based.

In the process of transforming its economy, China is also transforming the characteristics of its national leadership, in business and government. Few observers have recognized the way in which a leadership once characterized as old, conservative, and inward looking has advanced. For example, some of the most leading-edge communication, transportation, and energy technologies have been brought into play with a boldness that beggars belief.

And it is transforming its global presence as well. During the Tang Dynasty and for centuries thereafter, China saw itself as at the heart of the world. Then it was isolated. Now China sees itself as interconnected with the rest of the world. Any business with aspirations to global competitiveness must adopt a mindset that matches that of the Chinese in terms of openness and willingness to embrace the unfamiliar.

The Four Drivers of China's Economy

The current wave of China-related business books are primarily written with one of three goals: to explain China's emergence and its potential impact on the world economy; to show businesspeople how to enter China's economy and sell to its millions of consumers; or to provide guidance to business leaders on how to compete with their emerging Chinese rivals. In other words, they all tell part of the story—but they leave business leaders with an incomplete perspective.

In this book I will try to provide a holistic view of the Chinese business environment, looking at consumers, competitive enterprises, the government, integration with the rest of the world, and the ways these elements interact. I have also laid out a framework that puts together the different, often apparently contradictory, trajectories of China's future. This framework, which will be explicated in chapter 2, shows how change is taking place in a nonlinear fashion: some factors, such as Chinese entrepreneurship, are expanding exponentially, while others, such as the value of China's labor arbitrage, may be reaching a plateau.

To make sense of China's next decade, it is critical to grasp that there is no single driver of the nation's future. Instead, four very different drivers are pushing the country forward at once, all powerful, and all interacting with each other in unanticipated ways.

The first driver is an aspect of the country's economy and culture that I call *Open China*. The emerging potential of China's consumer markets is well known to outside producers, many of which, like General Motors, have already come to depend on these markets for their profitability. Unlike other leading economies in Asia, including Japan and South Korea, China began opening its markets to foreign companies at the very start of its economic reforms and it has opened them wider ever since.

At the same time, the Chinese people have rapidly advanced as consumers; the wealth created by China's growth has created a substantial middle class. Putting a precise number on the size of this segment of the population remains tricky, but however large it is, China's current middle class is a mere fraction of what it will become as hundreds of millions more people join its ranks over the next decade. After this honeymoon phase, the Chinese mass market will morph into a vast, highly differentiated and sophisticated, multitiered consumer economy capable of driving growth for Chinese and foreign companies alike. This growth trajectory represents a powerful short-term opportunity for major non-Chinese companies (for example, in helping to develop the country's retail sector) and a daunting long-term challenge in terms of maintaining market share.

This growth has also created an immense cultural transition from a largely rural country to a nation of cities. In the 1990s many companies had their hopes for China dashed because they were trying to sell urban-oriented products into a market where three-quarters of the people still lived in the countryside. Now around half live in urban areas. By 2020, this share will rise to 60 percent. This shift to an urbanized population means that China's markets, fundamentally different from ten years ago, will be transformed once again in the next decade. Urbanites need, and buy, fundamentally different types of products and services.

The second driver is *Competitive China*. Hundreds of thousands of new Chinese companies have made this country the world's most competitive business environment. Indeed, China is now the world's largest *and* fastest-growing source of entrepreneurial start-ups. It is also an incubator for large businesses, both foreign and home grown. Nearly 300,000 foreign-invested businesses have been established in China, vying to tap into the country's manufacturing base and reach its consumer and business markets.

And China is also becoming an innovation center for foreigners. The best of the world's companies have come here to transform themselves, gaining experience and capabilities in China that can be applied to their businesses worldwide. Meanwhile, many of China's leading entrepreneurs, like Li Ning, see themselves as natural global competitors. Companies such as the computer maker Lenovo, the white-goods firm Haier, and telecom equipment manufacturers Huawei and the Zhong Xing Telecommunication Equipment Company (ZTE) are building platforms of sufficient scale to take their businesses worldwide. They will be joined, in turn, by hundreds and then thousands more.

During the past fifteen years, global companies went to China primarliy to sell or manufacture goods. Over the next decade, international corporate leaders will go to China to integrate this vast market and sourcing hub with their global strategies and operations. Accomplishing this will require enormous leadership skills, within China and outside the country, especially at headquarters level.

Chinese producers will face unprecedented challenges of their own, including the challenge of sustainability. Since 1978, China's economic growth has been phenomenal, but also extremely inefficient. Driven by huge amounts of investment and fed by China's huge reservoir of rural labor, the focus has been on volume. But the related waste has been enormous, the environment has suffered, and consumer demand has been a secondary consideration. China's emphasis will switch toward creating a more efficient economy, as well as a more productive and competitive one. There will be a greater emphasis on demand as the main driver of growth versus investment, and on reducing the resources consumed per unit of output and the environmental impact, while raising technological and managerial standards.

The third driving force is *Official China*: the shifting direction and role of the government and Communist Party. The government has managed the liberalization of many parts of the economy, but it has maintained control over its strategic direction by retaining ownership of a core group of state-owned enterprises in the finance, communications, energy, resources, and media sectors. Contrary to the hopes of many foreign investors, Official China has no intention of letting go of these industries, and it will maintain tight control over those parts of the economy that it wishes to manage. As it faces the challenges of internal complexity and external engagement, it will remain nondemocratic while evolving toward a market-driven form of rule that, arguably, has never been seen on the world stage before.

One certainty is that economic liberalization will continue. There is a deep commitment within the government to continuing down the path China has followed for nearly thirty years. Part of the reason is that economic growth is a key foundation of legitimacy for China's government, and a major guarantor of political and social stability. Further, there is a deep belief that economic liberalization will raise China's position in the world, not just economically but also in terms of global leadership, reputation, and respect.

Many Chinese officials have internalized this aspiration. They have taken on responsibilities beyond their job descriptions, acting as the guiding hand in the creation of China as a world-leading country. Their interests extend beyond self-enrichment to the creation of national wealth and pride. This has been the motive behind building up the infrastructure necessary to economic development. It also means a long-term commitment to ensuring incremental economic development, as well as a willingness to experiment and collaborate across government agencies and with the private sector.

Evidence of this approach can be seen in the commitment to developing and running the large number of special economic zones that dot the country, especially along the coast. It is also visible in official attempts to prevent the emergence of an oligarchical tycoon class—such as that which dominated Russia in recent years—with a power base of its own independent from the Communist Party.

And it can be seen in the government's new level of external engagement. Starting in the 1950s, Mao cut China off from most of the world. Deng, when he launched China's economic reforms in the early 1990s, deliberately downplayed foreign relations, stressing that it was more important to focus on internal challenges. But the export-driven nature of China's growth means it must have trade relations with almost every country. The need for resources to fuel China's growth means that Chinese companies must source energy and raw materials from wherever they can find them. The Chinese government, like its citizens, has no choice but to reach out to the rest of the world.

And the world has no choice but to reach back. The fourth driving force is the *One World* in which China, like all other countries, is interdependent as never before. Globally connected power, communications, and transportation links now exist almost everywhere in China. The artifacts of the twenty-first-century global economy—KFC and McDonald's restaurants, Nokia phones and iPods, England's Premier League and MTV—are appearing in even the most remote Chinese cities. Although trade disputes, terrorism, and political tensions continue, the global geopolitical community will not go back to Cold War–era rivalries, or to the fragmented nationalism that preceded them. The nature of "one world" and the open, entrepreneurial business culture in China will reinforce each other in unexpected ways. No major player on the world stage can ignore China, and any company active in China will find itself increasingly interdependent with business in other parts of the world.

Of course, global integration remains far from complete. Any serious understanding of the current global economy must recognize the differences between China and the rest of the world, and limits of globalization in general. As Pankaj Ghemawat points out in *Redefining Global Strategy*,[11] most business activities remain country based, even when they can be conducted across borders. In China, given its size, this holds even more so: regions and provinces retain their distinct identities, with their own cuisines, customs, dialects, and sometimes languages. To use an extreme example, Hong Kong, despite more than a century and a half as an English colony, never ceased being Cantonese.

Together, the four drivers of change in China—Open China, Competitive China, Official China, and One World—will transform the way in which businesses operate everywhere. Managing supply chains, for example, will no longer mean simply seeking low-cost production in

China, but tapping the country's engineering and scientific capabilities for leading-edge research and development. Goods that are conceived, designed, and developed in China will be marketed to the rest of the world. Chinese companies, meanwhile, will increasingly go abroad to find new sources of technology and business skills, particularly for innovation, brand building, and access to international finance.

Developing Your Own Strategy

When you put all these pieces together, you see a complex business environment, unavoidable yet daunting—but also accessible for those who are prepared with flexible, observant, and engaged business strategies. China defies easy answers, but you can build the judgment and mindset needed to operate there, and by doing so, you can equip yourself better for business in the world at large.

Companies will have to embrace complexity to achieve success in China. No simple marketing or production strategy will fit all of a company's needs—the country and its dynamics are simply too varied. A strategy that works in the telecommunications sector in China will not necessarily work in computers; some alliances will be successful while others are not; a marketing strategy that works marvelously in one part of the country may fail miserably in another region. Despite all the business literature published on China, most authors and experts still treat this vast country in a facile way; they claim that one can "know" China after studying the business environment in a few major cities. That is like claiming to "know" the United States after working in New York, Washington, and Chicago.

Throughout the rest of this book, I will describe how to build the capabilities that business leaders need for developing an integrated China-global strategy. For example, you will learn how to tell which Chinese companies can provide the best alliances for particular purposes; what parts of the country to enter first; how to manage Chinese financing; and how to establish a trajectory for growth that benefits from the growth of the next wave of Chinese competitors. I will discuss flexible "footprints" for locating innovation, manufacturing, and services; the adaptation of brand names in China's many markets; and the integration of back-office functions between China and the rest of the world. You will also learn how success in China can be applied globally, using the market knowledge, networks of low-cost suppliers, and scientific talent that can be found there as a platform for reaching a worldwide scale.

The structure of this book is intended to help you apply this aspiration to your own business and situation. The first half explores each of the four main drivers of change in China and how they fit together.

Chapter 2, "Open China," explores the dynamics of the Chinese market—why it is expanding so rapidly and what this offers to companies, both Chinese and international. It briefly reviews the history of the last three decades to show just how important China's openness has been in shaping the opportunities, then turns to look at how China's markets will evolve over the next decade and beyond.

Chapter 3, "Entrepreneurial China," examines the different types of companies operating in China, and the nature of the competitive threat they offer to each other. Two conceptual frameworks—a *product market freedom* matrix and a *value-chain migration* model—are introduced to explore the amount and nature of competition that companies are likely to face, and the kinds of functions they can expect to run in their China operations over the next several years.

Chapter 4, "Official China," considers the role of the government and the Communist Party, the limits these two forces will put on China's movement toward being a fully market-driven economy, and how their changing priorities will shape the business environment over the next decade.

Chapter 5, "One World," pulls the threads of the previous three chapters together to show how the combination of China's market liberalization and the integration of China into global value chains has laid the groundwork for integrated global strategies—the strategies that will propel the most successful companies of the next few decades.

The second half of this book then looks more closely at this type of strategy, how to craft it, and how to build the capabilities you need to implement it.

Chapter 6, "Vision," describes the mindset—or strategic vision— that companies must develop to negotiate China's business environment over the next decade. It explains why a China orientation is also a global mindset; that if a company does not try to shape its global strategy in the light of its China strategy, not only will it likely lose out in markets around the world, but it will also face the prospect of underperforming within China.

Chapter 7, "Versatility," identifies the core capabilities companies must develop to realize their strategic vision. It highlights the need for flexibility, speed, and the ability to manage change, with a particular emphasis on the techniques used by China's most successful domestic companies and how they have used their home market advantage to build the foundations for international expansion.

Chapter 8, "Vigilance," discusses the type of leadership traits that corporate executives and managers will need to develop as they face the challenges of leading their businesses in China.

Chapter 9, "The Chinese Renaissance," is a small epilogue suggesting that what we are seeing is more than just an economy reemerging. China's revitalization could be as significant to the world as the great period in the early Tang Dynasty.

Throughout this book I recount the experiences of companies that have begun to develop their own versions of the China strategy. These include multinational companies such as Coca-Cola, IBM, KFC, Honeywell, and Nokia; and Chinese companies such as Huawei, ZTE, BYD, Haier, Li Ning, Dongxiang, Hengan, and Wanxiang. The companies that succeed the most will do so because they adopt a strategic mindset: not strategies for China alone but global strategies with China at their core.

In this sense, China is the first country that has become truly analogous to the United States in geo-economic terms. Because of the scale of the American market, and because of the global reach and power of American corporations, every truly global company must compete, at least in some form, in the U.S. market. The same will hold true in China. If a company ignores China, it cedes this region to its competitors. If a company enters China strategically, it builds an increasingly necessary base from which it can establish its competitive prowess.

My Own Story

The China Strategy draws on my experience from nearly two decades of working with business leaders in the country. I have worked with hundreds of global companies seeking to establish manufacturing or sourcing bases and penetrate the country's markets, and an equal number of Chinese companies aspiring to develop their management capabilities and go overseas. Being born in Hong Kong, then educated in the United States, has put me in the fortunate position of being able to incorporate insights from both management cultures. As a child and young adult, I was always interested in Chinese and world history, and after working in China, I began to study Chinese business history going back several centuries, in an effort to learn about the country's deeper commercial traditions and values. As a senior partner in Booz & Company and as the firm's chairman for Greater China, I can confirm that the business models and approaches in this book are practical; they have been developed and tested in work with many foreign and domestic companies, and found to meet the specific demands of a wide range of sectors and industries.

This book provides a series of frameworks that businesses can use to succeed in China. While case studies are used to illustrate key points, it is important to grasp the overall themes. Extrapolating from a small number of points to draw conclusions is always rash. Unfortunately, that is what many do when it comes to dealing with China—hence the willingness of observers to declare China to be everything from on the brink of collapse to the next superpower. Worse still, when things do not turn out as predicted on the basis of a handful of data points, China is declared to be incomprehensible.

What is needed instead is a sufficiently holistic picture of China— the Chinese context—that can explain what is happening and identify the driving forces determining its future. This is particularly important for corporate leaders. They need to know which elements of the vast amount of information and data on Chinese markets, customers, and competitors are relevant to their industry and must be monitored, and which they can safely ignore. Given China's size, knowledge will always be incomplete, meaning that executives must be aware of both what they know and what they do not know. In this way, when any major decision is taken, risk can be more accurately assessed.

My starting point for thinking about these issues was the early 1990s, shortly after I started practicing consulting in China. One of my first assignments was helping an American snack-food company that wanted to enter the Chinese market. Together, we looked at its competitors and their products. In addition to other international snack-food makers, there were Chinese, Taiwanese, Hong Kong, Singaporean, and Malaysian competitors. In short, although the market was nascent, there was already a phenomenal number of rivals to contend with. Clearly, China had already passed the stage where an outside company could easily enter, find a partner to help it get established, and expect a free run at the market.

It struck me that the Chinese government played a very small role in saying what companies could or could not do. There were no rules insisting that foreign companies had to have local partners, or restrictions on what could or could not be sold, as long as they complied with baisc practices for health and hygiene.

This was very different from what I had expected. During my years away, I had often heard that running any business in China was a nightmare. The key to any kind of progress was *guanxi*, the Chinese word for connections. Yet here was a totally contradictory example: what business people needed was a good product, strong marketing and brand strategies, the ability to distribute goods, and a sound understanding of local consumers; officials were nowhere in sight. True, success would require coping with ferocious competition, but the nature of the challenge was broadly similar to that which would face a snack-food company anywhere in the world.

Unfortunately, when I tried to have a telephone installed in my office, I found myself confronted with a very different China. Not only was the installation fee huge, but the whole process took six months. The service was awful and support was nonexistent. The main reason for this was that China's only telecommunications operator then was not even a company, but an arm of what was at that time called the Ministry of Posts and Telecommunications. Immune from competition, unaccountable to consumers, and without the need to make profits, it could safely ignore the needs of businesspeople coming in from overseas (and Chinese businesspeople as well).

So there I was, struggling to reconcile these two very different impressions. On the one hand I saw a place with a very open, highly competitive consumer goods sector, where international companies had to bring their top people and best-in-class capabilities to succeed. And on the other hand I saw a totally closed, rigidly controlled telecommunications sector, with just one player, whose products and services were poor and expensive.

Later, as I was increasingly invited to conferences around the world to talk about China, I realized that it made no sense to talk about what was going on there as a series of isolated cases or examples. I had to put what was happening into a framework that could explain these apparent contradictions. My attention focused on two key trends: the government's ongoing deregulation of sector after sector of the economy and the way in which multinational companies were beginning to move more elements of their value chains to China. From these I developed the conceptual frameworks—*product market freedom* and *value-chain migration*—that linked internal changes in China with the arrival of foreign multinationals from around the world.

The frameworks, and the four driving forces that underlie change in China, have helped me and many others grasp the overall context of this country and its implications for particular businesses. With an understanding of these dynamics, corporate leaders can position themselves not just to succeed in China, but to be part of the great renaissance now unfolding there—a renaissance that will change the world.

CHAPTER 2

Open China

AFTER THIRTY YEARS of opening and liberalizing its economy, nowhere else, not even among the mature markets of Japan, Europe, and the United States, offers the same extraordinary range of brands and products as China. If you doubt this, step into a convenience store in, say, Shanghai, Dalian, or Shenzhen. Accompanying the Western products Coke, Pepsi, and Schweppes there are Japanese soft drinks made by Suntory, Kirin, and Sapporo, Taiwanese flavors under the Uni-President label, and Hong Kong brands such as Vitasoy. Alongside the bottled waters, colas, and beers are teas, coffees, and soya milk drinks, plus ones made from fruits unfamiliar to most foreigners. Chinese companies make their own versions of every international flavor—and many flavors that are not produced elsewhere.

Outside, on the newsstands, are Chinese magazines—and Chinese editions of such familiar global titles as *Cosmopolitan*, *Vogue*, and *Elle*. Driving on the streets are locally manufactured vehicles from almost every global carmaker—General Motors (GM) and Ford, Toyota and Honda, Volkswagen (VW) and its subsidiary Audi, BMW and Mercedes, Citroën and Hyundai—plus a host of local auto brands, including Chery, Geely, Brilliance, and Great Wall. Step inside a department store and there's a proliferation of labels and choices: from sportswear to electronic goods, handbags to massage equipment, foreign to local, high end to low end, and everything in between. Even someone accustomed to American or European superstores might find it a bit daunting; but for most of the local patrons in cities such as Shenyang, Wuhan, and Changsha, it's a remarkable change from the sparsely stocked, perfunctorily managed shops they patronized just a decade ago.

At first glance, for global consumer-oriented companies, this would seem to be the realization of a dream. For years, they have looked forward to the rise of the mythical "land of one billion-plus consumers"—new to the middle class, eager for new products, ready to be sold to. And indeed, for some companies the last decade has been an extraordinary and exciting time, and in many cases a prosperous one. Executives who argued in the 1990s that China's markets for their goods would rise exponentially were vindicated. The old perception of China as a poor country with a closed economy has become obsolete.

To be sure, the ability of many Chinese to join the consumer economy is still restricted by the country's overall low per capita income, especially away from the largest and wealthiest metropolitan centers. But now that China's consumer market has been unlocked, it cannot be reversed. Since the start of the 1990s, annual retail sales have increased more than fifteenfold, from around $100 billion to more than $1.6 trillion by the end of 2008. This represented about one-third of sales in the United States during this period.[1] That is not a one-time phenomenon; it is here to stay.

Yet the Chinese consumer market is more complex than people expect, and the challenges to achieving profitability are growing. For new openness is bringing with it phenomenal competition, abrupt rises and falls in market share for both new and established products, and almost zero brand loyalty. The experience of companies like KFC suggests that the new Chinese consumers are rapidly becoming as diverse in their tastes and needs, and as demanding and fickle, as their Western counterparts. They cannot be taken for granted.

Anatomy of an Open Market

The big winners in open China are the consumers themselves. They are now choosing from a cornucopia of goods in almost every product category, from every corner of the world, all competing for their attention, and many of them sold at rock-bottom prices.

For companies trying to reach these consumers, the prospects vary by industry. Although the markets for certain types of goods rival and sometimes surpass other of the world's largest consumer markets, this has not been true in every sector. The size of the market for mobile phones and television sets may be comparable among China, the United States, and Europe, but for products that call for additional discretionary spending, such as DVD players, Chinese sales levels remain below those in developed-country markets (see exhibit 2-1). In some sectors, sales are rapidly rising. In 2009, auto unit sales in China exceeded those in the United States for the first time.

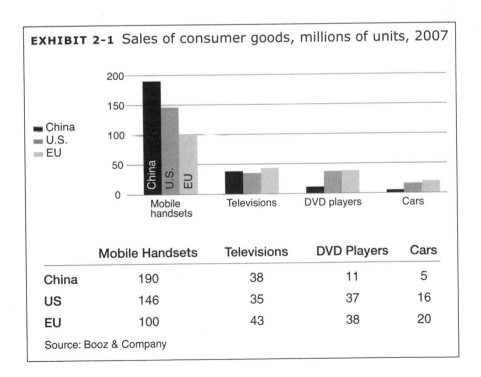

EXHIBIT 2-1 Sales of consumer goods, millions of units, 2007

	Mobile Handsets	Televisions	DVD Players	Cars
China	190	38	11	5
US	146	35	37	16
EU	100	43	38	20

Source: Booz & Company

Since the early 1990s, and especially since the early 2000s, the markets for various types of goods have experienced S-curve-shaped periods of growth. Three representative examples, from three very different industries, are the increase in mobile-phone subscriptions, the value of home mortgage loans, and sedan sales (see exhibit 2-2).

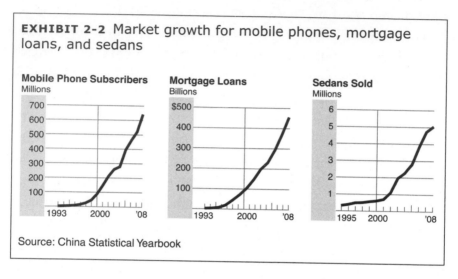

EXHIBIT 2-2 Market growth for mobile phones, mortgage loans, and sedans

Source: China Statistical Yearbook

Toward the end of the 1990s, China had 43 million mobile-phone subscribers, up from just a million six years earlier.[2] At the time, that seemed to be an impressive achievement, but what came next was unprecedented. The government reorganized the telecommunications industry, pitting China Mobile directly against the country's other mobile operator, China Unicom. Both companies slashed their tariffs and, helped by a liberal issuance of handset manufacturing licenses and heavy competition among foreign equipment suppliers, consumers found themselves presented with an irresistible combination of cheap phones, ultralow tariffs, and a state-of-the-art nationwide network. Better still, after years of having to endure long waiting lists, drawn-out bureaucratic procedures, and big up-front fees to get fixed lines, now all anyone had to do to get a phone was walk into a shop and sign up. Total subscribers increased more than tenfold to pass 500 million in 2007; by mid-2009, the number was up to 687 million.

The mortgage-loan market took off at the same time. In 1998, China's government reformed its urban housing policy. Until then, almost everyone's apartment was owned by the enterprise or organization that employed them; households were allocated a home for which they paid a token rent. The government, looking to free enterprises of their welfare burden, liberalized the housing market, jump-starting the process by offering city dwellers the option of buying their homes from their employers at giveaway prices. Overnight, the mortgage-loan industry was born. During the next decade, sales of residential floor space increased nearly tenfold, from around 80 million square meters to 700 million square meters.[3] In 2008, as the economy slowed in the wake of the global financial crisis, sales dropped. But the overall trend for the next decade remains strong growth: by 2020, China's urban population is expected to grow from 600 million to 800 million and all of its new urban residents will need somewhere to live.

As with mobile phones and mortgages, China's car-sales surge was driven by regulatory change and a corresponding surge in supply. In the early 2000s, as a succession of Sino-foreign joint ventures and independent Chinese auto firms invested in production capacity, the government allowed banks to offer auto loans and the carmakers to set up auto finance companies. Annual motor vehicle sales rose from around half a million in the late 1990s to more than 9 million by 2008. In January 2009, for the first time in history, monthly automobile sales in China surpassed those in the United States. And just after midyear, the China Association of Automobile Manufacturers increased its forecast for total vehicle sales for the year from 10 million to 12 million. Moreover, with manufacturers lowering prices, expanding their model ranges, and continuing to expand production capacity, prospective buyers will have both more lower-cost cars and more cars overall to choose from through the next decade.

In other sectors, profitability remains elusive. While survey after survey has found revenues and profits gradually rising, many businesses continue to struggle to reach the margins they would like. This includes sellers of inexpensive goods that almost every consumer can afford, and those that have operated in China for a long time.

Take Coca-Cola. It first entered China in 1927, then retreated during the early Communist years. It re-entered in 1979, just months after Deng ascended to power and launched his program of economic reforms, and ahead of its global rival, Pepsi. Since then, Coke has invested more than $1.3 billion, mostly on bottling infrastructure (through its joint ventures with bottlers, it has thirty-six bottling plants) and other facilities, including an $80 million headquarters and R&D center in Shanghai—one of six worldwide. Between 2009 and 2012, Coca-Cola is planning to invest an additional $2 billion in China. These investments will involve factory sites, production facilities, route-to-market supply-chain channels, product development, and marketing.

Over the years, Coke's sales have risen continuously, giving it almost one-third of China's market for nonalcoholic beverages. Like the sellers of cars and mobile phones, the company has recorded particularly strong growth in the last five years, with annual volume doubling to more than 1 billion unit cases—5.7 billion liters—making China its third-largest market by volume worldwide, after the United States and Mexico.

But although profitable, Coke's margins are thinner than its margins in the United States. Coca-Cola's Chinese business is being squeezed on all sides. A fragmented retail market—it estimates the number of outlets at somewhere between 7 million and 12 million—combined with a state monopoly over television advertising means that marketing and distribution costs are high. Competition from international and domestic rivals is ferocious and the competitive landscape is complicated. While it competes with Pepsi in the carbonated drink segment, Coca-Cola also faces off in the noncarbonated categories against local and Taiwanese brands, such as Kangshifu (Tinghsin), Wahaha Uni-President, and Wanglaoji. As a result, Coke needs to sell its drinks in China for among the lowest prices anywhere in the world. And with every competitor investing in capacity and clawing for market share, price competition will probably become even more intense. (Coca-Cola, as we'll see in later chapters, has also responded to this challenge by trying to acquire local Chinese brands.)

In other sectors companies face similarly fierce competition and dynamic markets. Their fortunes can rise and fall with astonishing speed. Take the car market: VW, after dominating throughout the 1990s, with a market share of more than 50 percent, saw its share drop rapidly and its performance slump into the red in the early 2000s. It was initially displaced as the market leader by GM, whose market share rose as it built a highly profitable joint venture with one of the country's largest automakers, Shanghai Automotive Industry Corp.— a company that also has a joint venture with VW. By 2008, GM was in turn finding itself eclipsed by Toyota, long regarded as a struggling latecomer, after the Japanese company brought a second plant into operation in the southern city of Guangzhou. Within a year, however, Toyota was also struggling, with reports suggesting it had lost half its market share in the first half of 2009 after failing to upgrade its models quickly enough to satisfy the demands of Chinese buyers.[4] A senior executive from a large Chinese automobile maker told me later that year that "the huge profit era of the Chinese automotive industry is now gone, because of intense competition."

Breathing down the necks of all the big international motor vehicle companies are China's own independent carmakers, whose share of the market rose from 20 percent in 2004 to about 29 percent in mid-2009. The largest of these companies, with 7 to 8 percent of the market, is Chery Auto—a relative newcomer, founded in 1997, which has already established itself as China's top car exporter. Potentially even more threatening to the established automakers is Shenzhen-based BYD. (Its initials stand for "build your dream.") Primarily a maker of mobile-phone batteries—and a successful one, with 130,000 employees and revenues of $3.1 billion—BYD decided to take on the automotive market with an electric car. It launched its first model in late 2008, two years ahead of the expected launch of

GM's Volt, with a car priced at just over half of the Volt's targeted price, and with a greater range. That same year, BYD received a major boost when a company owned by Warren Buffett bought a 10 percent stake for $230 million. (BYD's story is examined in more detail in chapter 8.)

As upstart entrants, BYD, Chery, and other Chinese carmakers face major challenges. BYD only sold its first car, a gasoline-fueled model, in 2005, and Chery only exports about 100,000 units a year, all to developing countries. But they have the potential to reshape China's automotive market, and beyond that, international markets—especially given the global restructuring of the industry that has to occur over the next decade. They will start by building scale at home, producing low-priced vehicles, then by leveraging domestic volume as the jumping-off point for international expansion. The Chinese government is likely to support these companies.

Given this combination of official goals and a consumer market that cannot support all of the companies now present, China's auto industry will inevitably undergo a major restructuring. When that will be is impossible to know. Car sales resumed after a brief slump in the latter half of 2008 and China has now become the world's largest automobile market. Sales are certain to continue growing through the 2010s, and automakers will continue to invest as long as they believe they can emerge as one of the eventual winners. At the same time, Chinese competition and the global financial crisis could accelerate consolidation in this industry, especially if foreign carmakers, particularly the American ones, find themselves distracted or put out of business by events in their home markets.

The Sources of Openness

One major but often unnoticed factor in the growth of China's consumer markets—and its instability and ferocious competitiveness as well—is the country's openness to foreign business. The government has allowed non-Chinese companies to set up manufacturing operations and sell freely in many sectors, and growing numbers of consumers not only welcome this variety of goods regardless of the country of origin of their makers, but consider it a symbol of their own increasing prosperity.

This openness has created ripe conditions for entry into many of China's industry sectors, both for foreign companies and new Chinese companies. Investment has surged into almost every industry, coming from both established players and total newcomers. Different sectors have different stories to tell, but for a high proportion of those making or selling consumer goods, the big picture remains the same: delayed returns on investment; strong downward price pressure; far higher costs than expected for many functions, especially marketing and distribution; and, a result of all of these, lower margins.

We've just seen how the world's most established automakers are finding themselves confronted by previously unknown Chinese competitors. In sportswear, Li Ning, Dongxiang, and Anta are credible threats to Adidas and Nike. Huawei and ZTE, both telecom equipment makers based in Shenzhen, used the growth of China's communications infrastructure to build the domestic volume necessary to launch their own equipment businesses worldwide. Their aggressive pricing, which accelerated a commoditization of many elements of the telecommunications industry, played a major role in driving a global consolidation that led to Alcatel's acquisition of Lucent and the merger of Nokia's and Siemens's equipment-making divisions. Over the next decade or two, the presence of Chinese companies can be expected to make restructuring more likely in a wide range of other industries— among them automotive, shipbuilding, chemicals, energy, information technology and, possibly, aerospace.

To understand the potential and the complexity of China's markets, one must therefore understand the nature of this openness and how it affects the trajectory of business development. Only those who see it clearly can formulate a China strategy that uses these markets to create organizational capabilities that can be applied globally. There are four ever-changing dimensions of openness to consider:

1. Openness to outsiders: the arrival and role of overseas investment in China.
2. Regional markets: the growth trajectories of geographic market development within China.
3. Improved distribution: developing more and better retail channels and the infrastructure necessary to support them.
4. Consumer culture: the evolution of a demanding and fickle population of purchasers.

These four dimensions can guide companies as to what to expect upon entering China, where to target their efforts, how to plan their distribution, and what sort of consumer markets may emerge.

1. Openness to Outsiders

When Deng Xiaoping launched his economic reforms in the late 1970s and early 1980s, he had no grand vision of making the country join the global economy. Indeed, what happened next was one of the great ironies in recent commercial history. Deng and his fellow officials wanted the opposite of globalization. They wanted to acquire technology and know-how from abroad, while minimizing China's exposure to outside influence. Hence the decision to try and concentrate foreign investment in a handful of "special economic zones" that were open to the world, but largely closed to the rest of China. Access to these zones was limited to those who worked within them.

The great liftoff in foreign investment only came in the 1990s. Its ignition point can be traced precisely to 1992—when Deng Xiaoping undertook what Chinese call his "southern tour." Traveling to Shenzhen and then Shanghai, he urged officials to relaunch and expand China's economic reforms that had faltered after the suppression of the student-led democracy movement of 1989. His call was taken up across the country, especially by Zhu Rongji, the senior Party official who was China's single most influential voice on the economy during the past twenty years. On Zhu's watch, first as vice premier and then as premier, China undertook or began all of the most significant reforms that have created the economy we see today. Zhu took China into the World Trade Organization (WTO); he privatized the country's housing stock; he launched the overhaul of the country's financial system; and most astonishingly of all, he oversaw the biggest single example of "creative destruction" the world has seen: the wholesale closure of much of China's state-owned sector in the late 1990s and early 2000s, and the creation in its place of a private sector. [5]

This latter change, in which tens of thousands of state-owned companies were closed and some 30 million workers lost their jobs, laid the foundations for today's more productive economy. Those parts of the state sector that survived are strongly profitable—among them earning more than $200 billion in 2007, the equivalent of well over 6 percent of GDP. (Before the change, their earnings had been about 0.5 percent.) Still more significant was the boost this removal of deadwood gave to the private sector. Forced to find work wherever they could, most of the workers who lost their jobs ended up in private enterprises. In 1997, the urban private sector employed 24 million people; a decade later, that had risen to nearly 80 million.[6]

Zhu focused on allowing market forces to determine the direction of development rather than using government intervention. This explains why, from the early 1990s onward, he attached such importance to WTO entry: the best way to improve the performance of Chinese companies, he reasoned, was to expose them to the best practices and competitive challenge of foreign companies. It also helps explain why foreign investment started arriving in China in large volumes in the mid-1990s. Although China had first opened its doors to foreign companies at the end

EXHIBIT 2-3 Foreign direct investment into China, 1985–2008, $ billions

1985	2.0	1991	4.4	1997	45.3	2003	53.5
1986	2.2	1992	11.0	1998	45.5	2004	60.6
1987	2.3	1993	27.5	1999	40.3	2005	60.3
1988	3.2	1994	33.8	2000	40.7	2006	63.0
1989	3.4	1995	37.5	2001	46.9	2007	74.8
1990	3.5	1996	41.7	2002	52.7	2008	92.4

Source: National Bureau of Statistics, Ministry of Commerce[7]

of the 1970s, the true influx of foreign capital only began in 1992, rising to a record high in 2008 of more than $90 billion (see exhibit 2-3).

For cities and towns along China's southern and eastern coasts, often with little more to offer than land and unskilled labor, attracting foreign investment became the quickest and easiest way to develop. In these regions, especially in the 1990s, keeping this money arriving became a major imperative—to spearhead growth, create jobs, help upgrade infrastructure, boost exports, earn hard currency, obtain technology, and introduce new managerial practices. As growth surged, more sectors were opened and more economic development zones were built. Foreign companies were offered more tax breaks and granted more freedom, to entice them to operate wholly owned businesses instead of the joint ventures the government had first required.

For foreign manufacturers in particular, the freedom to operate on their own terms was a major plus. The benefits of China's low-cost

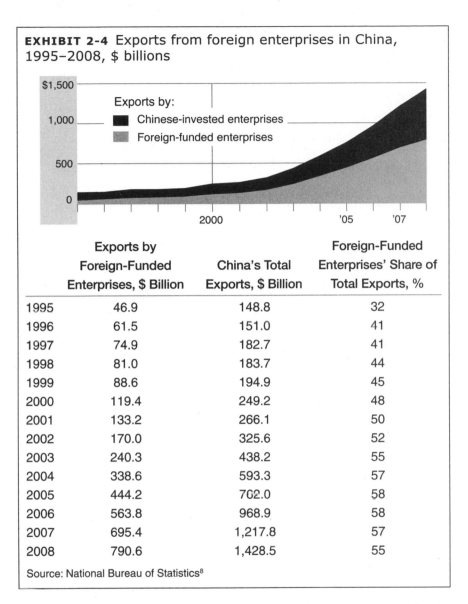

EXHIBIT 2-4 Exports from foreign enterprises in China, 1995–2008, $ billions

	Exports by Foreign-Funded Enterprises, $ Billion	China's Total Exports, $ Billion	Foreign-Funded Enterprises' Share of Total Exports, %
1995	46.9	148.8	32
1996	61.5	151.0	41
1997	74.9	182.7	41
1998	81.0	183.7	44
1999	88.6	194.9	45
2000	119.4	249.2	48
2001	133.2	266.1	50
2002	170.0	325.6	52
2003	240.3	438.2	55
2004	338.6	593.3	57
2005	444.2	702.0	58
2006	563.8	968.9	58
2007	695.4	1,217.8	57
2008	790.6	1,428.5	55

Source: National Bureau of Statistics[8]

manufacturing base more than compensated for their frustrations in trying to sell into China's fragmented and hard-to-penetrate markets. As foreign investment poured in, China was transformed into one of the world's leading exporters. Foreign-owned companies displaced domestic ones as the main source of Chinese exports, with their share of exports rising to nearly 60 percent (see exhibit 2-4).

Such figures are a tribute to Chinese openness—and a rebuke to those around the world, who criticize China for resorting to unfair trade practices. Chinese companies certainly play a substantial role in producing the country's trade surplus, but foreign companies have played a larger role, taking advantage of China's openness and low costs to improve their competitiveness. Along the way, China has created an economy that although still closed in many respects, is far more open than those of its neighbors, Japan and South Korea, and many other developed countries. For example, China has allowed several foreign auto brands, including BMW and Mercedes-Benz, onto procurement lists for government vehicles; other countries, including Korea and Japan, have been much more restrictive at times.

As for China's government leaders, the liberalization of China's economy and the opening of its borders to foreign companies generated unforeseen consequences. Arguably the most significant of these was the degree to which foreign companies and their ideas and practices penetrated the Chinese economy. Gradually, the Chinese leaders have come to accept the fact that this has benefited China. In the short term, it has brought investment, created jobs and demand, boosted trade, and generally stimulated the economy; in the long term, it exposed Chinese companies to competition and the best practices of global businesses. The best Chinese managers may go and work for multinational companies, but many will also return and work for Chinese companies, or establish their own start-ups, using the skills they have acquired and passing them on to others in the process. Openness has also brought foreign goods to China, which in turn has encouraged Chinese companies to produce their own versions.

And yet, the Chinese economy may be at a new point of transition, becoming more challenging. Foreign companies expecting a similar welcome to that of the previous fifteen years will find some major changes—and could be disappointed. It is not that China will close its economy; along with the United States, it has been, and will continue to be, one of the greatest beneficiaries of the tide of globalization that swept across the world in the past twenty years. Foreign investment will remain lucrative in China in the years to come, perhaps more so than ever, and global capital will continue to be drawn there. In their book *Merge Ahead,* Booz & Company partners Gerald Adolph and Justin Pettit say that China is "indispensable for multinationals to enter,"[9] and it remains one of the most attractive investment markets in the world.

But foreign capital will no longer play the same kind of key enabling role to China's transformation. The big changes, which outside investment helped facilitate, have now taken place. China has most of the resources that it lacked at the start of the 1990s, including money and know-how, necessary to develop its economy. Of course, there remain elements in short supply, such as certain technologies and areas of expertise. But with the economy largely transformed, and its two weakest areas—state-owned enterprise and the banking system—utterly unrecognizable from just fifteen years ago, the greatest era of foreign investment's impact is at an end. Foreign companies arriving now (or looking to expand their existing investments) will do so in a crowded, competitive environment, where they can expect fewer incentives, such as tax and land breaks, than they received in the past.

2. Regional Markets

If the golden era for foreign investment in China is ending, the golden era of its markets has barely begun. During the 1990s, countless companies arrived in China intent on selling their products in the country's vast consumer markets. Many were disappointed. Despite heavy investment, returns were pitifully low in many sectors. Among the many casualties were virtually every foreign brewer, various electronic consumer-goods makers, automakers, including General Motors, and a host of other companies that mistakenly thought "China's emerging middle class"— potentially tens of millions of new customers—was ready for them.

EXHIBIT 2-5 The three major consumer regions

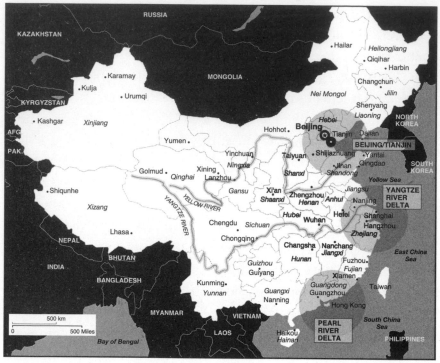

Until now, the reality of China's consumer markets was very different from the dream. But oddly enough, just at the moment that China's growth seems to have slowed, its consumer population is finally ready to emerge in force. The steep slope of an S curve of demand is increasingly apparent, in which rising consumer interest snowballs—not for any single product, but for the total population of accessible consumers in China.

Currently, three areas stand out as the primary places with significant consumer potential (see exhibit 2-5):

- The Yangtze River Delta region, centered on Shanghai, with a population of just more than 80 million and a GDP of around Rmb4.5 trillion, or about US$660 billion (roughly comparable to that of Turkey, Poland, or the U.S. state of Illinois).

- The Pearl River Delta, centered on the axis between Guangzhou and Shenzhen, with a population approaching 45 million and a GDP of Rmb2.5 trillion, or about US$365 billion (roughly comparable to that of Greece or Massachusetts).
- The Beijing-Tianjin region, often referred to as the Bohai Sea region, with a population of around 25 million and a GDP of around Rmb2 trillion, or about US$290 billion (roughly comparable to that of Ireland, South Africa, or Maryland).

Most foreign companies looking to sell their goods into China concentrate their efforts in these three regions, for several reasons. They account for almost half of China's GDP and have relatively high per capita GDP, around US$5,000–6,500.[10] Although there are many other middle-income households in cities across China, in the past they have remained too dispersed to form markets that are readily reachable by most businesses, especially foreign ones.

But that will change. One key factor in pushing China's consumer markets on a relentless growth trajectory through the next decade is urbanization, driven by the continued migration of people from rural areas to urban centers (see exhibit 2-6).

Since 2000, the urban population has grown by more than 125 million people. That's a large figure, but it's barely more than half of what we will see in the next decade. By 2020, another 200-million-plus people will be living in cities, making the urban population 56 percent of China's total. These national figures don't fully reveal the most recent upheavals. In the provinces of east China, urbanization is far higher (at 55 percent of the population) than the center of the country (40 percent) or the west (just above 35 percent).

According to the World Bank, the return on labor in services is around three times that of agriculture; in industry, it is around ten times as much. In other words, there is no better way of generating economic growth and raising per capita income than generating industrial jobs for rural inhabitants. That's exactly what happened in

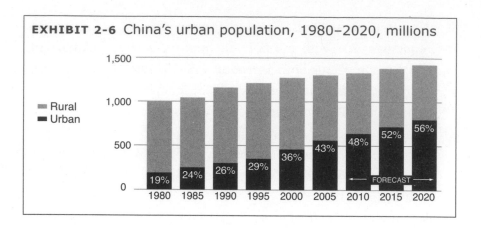

EXHIBIT 2-6 China's urban population, 1980–2020, millions

China during the last two decades, as peasants left their fields to work in the factories of the eastern and southern coasts. And it will continue to happen in the coming years, with many new urban residents in central and eastern China.[12]

The switch from being a predominantly rural to a predominantly urban population will have an impact on almost every aspect of Chinese life. A massive new wave of people will be lifted from poverty— probably far more in the next few years than in the past few decades. And after 5,000 years of being a predominantly rural, agricultural country, China will find itself a country of city dwellers virtually overnight. The overall impact of this new urban prosperity on the markets of open China will be enormous; and the enormity is made even clearer by looking at the breakdown of the country's communities by size.

Since the start of the 1990s, the most prosperous segment of the population has been concentrated in the largest metropolitan areas of China's coastal regions and their immediate hinterlands. Shanghai, Beijing, Guangzhou, and Shenzhen are typically identified as the "big four": the largest cities with the highest income, largest population base, and largest GDP scale.

Following this is a group of about twenty "tier-two" cities. These are mega cities in their own right, home to between 4 and 32 million people each. (Chongqing is the largest, but only 6 of its 32 million residents are urban.) These include such major centers as Dongguan, Nanjing, Wuhan, Hangzhou, Shenyang, and Harbin. This group also includes four smaller cities—Zhungshow, Xiamen, Changzhou, and Zhuhai—whose lower populations are offset by their higher per capita GDP.

During the course of the 1990s and 2000s, a larger market, particularly for consumer goods made by domestic manufacturers, was added in so-called third-tier "emerging middle class" cities. These include cities like Dalian, Qingdao, Shantou, Kunming, Zibo, Huizhou, Shijiazhuang, Fuzhou, and Changsha, many of them provincial capitals, and all with between 2 and 4 million inhabitants. When people talk of China's middle classes, they are referring to the average population of these first three tiers.

But the vast majority of the current urban population live in the next two tiers. Tier four, the "next wave," comprises about 140 cities with populations of 1 million to 2 million. And there are more than 400 cities in tiers five and six. These are the rural and remote cities, respectively, with populations of 500,000 to 1 million.[13] The so-far elusive market of hundreds of millions of Chinese consumers will be found in tiers four through six (see exhibit 2-7).

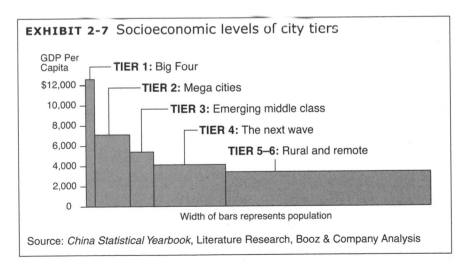

EXHIBIT 2-7 Socioeconomic levels of city tiers

GDP Per Capita

TIER 1: Big Four
TIER 2: Mega cities
TIER 3: Emerging middle class
TIER 4: The next wave
TIER 5–6: Rural and remote

$12,000
10,000
8,000
6,000
4,000
2,000
0

Width of bars represents population

Source: *China Statistical Yearbook*, Literature Research, Booz & Company Analysis

Most of these cities can be expected to grow, especially those outside the Yangtze River Delta, Pearl River Delta, and Beijing-Tianjin regions. As these cities grow in clusters, they will evolve into new regions of relative wealth and prominence. To spread growth more evenly around the country, the government is encouraging the creation of a series of new city clusters. They are located in the northeast, around southern and central Liaoning province; around Qingdao and the other cities of the Shandong Peninsula on the north China coast; on the southern Fujian coast, opposite Taiwan; in the middle reaches of the Yangtze, around Wuhan; around Chongqing, on the upper reaches of the Yangtze, and its neighbor, Chengdu, the capital of Sichuan, and in central Shaanxi province, around Xian.

Jinjiang, in the southern part of the Fujian province, is a good example of this extraordinary growth. Its population of 1.02 million people places it solidly in tier three. It is home to many thriving Chinese manufacturers and branded companies, including sports shoe and apparel makers such as Anta and X-Step; apparel companies such as 361 Degrees, Jiumuwang, and Septwolves; and Hengan, China's leading paper products company and a key competitor to Kimberly-Clark and Procter & Gamble.

Expressways linking many of these new city clusters are already in place; expanded rail links should follow in the next ten to twenty years. Almost all of these regions have some form of industrial advantage already, and have attracted significant levels of foreign investment, if not at the same volume as along the coast. Some multinational companies are expanding into these markets, with much depending on the type and degree of distribution and support they need. These companies include Coca-Cola, which markets its products in every part of China; KFC, with restaurants in more than 450 cities, including most of the tier-three cities; and Procter & Gamble, which has built China's most developed distribution network for fast-moving consumer goods.

For most multinationals, therefore, a crucial question is where and at what rate other concentrations are being formed beyond the "big three" regions, and when these new markets will become sizable enough to merit attention.

The ability to anticipate and reach consumers in tiers three and four (and more rural areas) will determine how successful a company can be in China over the next decade. Just since 2008, driven by increasing government incentives and residential income growth, demand is growing in these areas for consumer electronics, entertainment, and travel—with car and house purchases on the agenda for many families in the next several years. A sharply honed sense of timing will be just as important: go too early and a lot of money will be wasted; enter too late and competitors will have already established themselves.

3. Improved Distribution

If China's urban population, especially in its third- and fourth-tier cities, is set to expand dramatically in the next decade, how will companies reach those markets? The government has begun to address this question, identifying distribution as a key area for improvement. Over the past fifteen years, it has made massive investments in transportation infrastructure, especially roads.

At the start of the 1990s, China had just under 200 miles of expressways. It now has over 40,000 miles. Almost all of its major cities have new or totally rebuilt airports. And investment in its railway system, after lagging badly for most of the last two decades, is being rectified—after just adding some 12,000 miles of track between 1990 and 2008, another 7,500 miles will be laid by the end of 2010 (see exhibit 2-8).

China has also liberalized its distribution sector to a large degree. It has opened road transport and other logistics industries to foreign companies, and it has started to encourage the consolidation of numerous, small domestic transport companies into a few integrated giants with nationwide reach and corresponding economies of scale. Admittedly, progress on the latter front has been slow. Trucking companies in

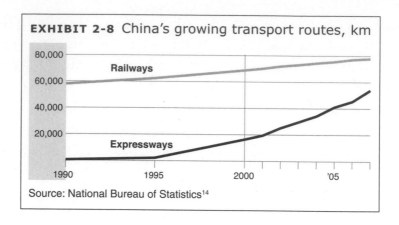

EXHIBIT 2-8 China's growing transport routes, km

Source: National Bureau of Statistics[14]

particular have proliferated as the expressway network has grown. And at both a central and local level there remains a tendency to focus on developing "hard" infrastructure, such as highways and logistics parks, rather than the equally important forms of "soft" infrastructure: communications, software (for managing logistics, for example), and managerial capabilities.

The current expressway network's greatest shortcoming is that it largely connects only cities with populations of half a million or more. Most third- and fourth-tier cities are reachable only by standard highways. But this too will change, with the 7-9-18 scheme—the most ambitious road-building project in world history—comprising seven expressways starting in Beijing, nine north-south routes, and eighteen east-west routes. With a total investment of $250 billion, its 53,000 miles will link all of China's cites with a population of 200,000 or more by the time it is completed in the 2030s.

Meanwhile, the country is at the start of a retail revolution. Currently, the vast majority of shopping outlets remain the market stalls, corner shops, and kiosks used by most Chinese citizens to buy everyday necessities. But this is changing. The change began in 2001, when China joined the World Trade Organization and foreign retailers and wholesalers were granted permission to operate anywhere in China. There has since been an explosion in shopping options, with both domestic and foreign retailers involved. Supermarkets, twenty-four-hour convenience stores, and chains of all sizes are spreading within larger cities, led by international companies such as Carrefour (with about 140 individual stores), Wal-Mart (with about 150 stores), and a few Chinese retailers such as the electronic goods seller GOME (with more than 1,300 outlets) and Suning (with more than 800 stores).

The rapid growth of retail chains, and their correspondingly more sophisticated formats, have compelled distributors to meet their customers' new needs. This represents a major improvement in the rapid movement of consumer goods and food, especially if the distributors can deliver direct to the stores themselves, or to the retail chains' distribution centers. That improvement is still relatively weak; it is held back by the highly fragmented and inefficient nature of China's retail, transport, and logistics industries. In Europe and America, logistics costs are the equivalent of less than 10 percent of GDP; in China, the figure is roughly double that.

Given the amount of time and money that it takes to build a distribution network, many companies have opted to outsource theirs. This will make sense as long as China's transport and logistics sectors remain fragmented, and until these sectors gain experience in managing modern logistics systems. But that day will come and, as often happens in China, it may transform with dizzying speed.

One company widely acknowledged to have well-developed retail distribution structures and processes is Procter & Gamble (P&G). It entered China in the 1980s and first developed a distribution network for shampoo. Then, P&G added other products one by one, building on its experience both in reaching markets across the country and running marketing campaigns to support the launch of each new category of goods.

Another success story is KFC, the most successful restaurant chain in China—foreign or domestic. This is, of course, the same chain as the American KFC, with a signature dish of fried chicken. Since arriving in 1987, it has set up more than 2,900 restaurants in 450 cities, with around 300 new outlets opening each year. McDonald's, its biggest rival, has less than half that total, and is only adding new locations at less than half KFC's rate. With a turnover of around $2 billion, China is KFC's second-largest market after the United States, and its largest source of earnings growth. KFC's parent, Yum! Brands, does not publicly reveal the chain's profitability. But Sam Su, the company leader who oversaw KFC's successes through its two-decade presence in China, and who now heads up Yum!'s operations in the country, pointed out recently that the top brand in a sector typically enjoys the best margins, that KFC is clearly the fast-food leader in China, and that he is "very happy" with the amount of money KFC is making.[15]

There are several factors behind KFC's success in China. First, it has managed to build a strong supply chain. Although the decision to do this may have been easy to make, implementing it was another matter. Like Procter & Gamble, KFC spent a long time—nearly a decade—figuring out its basic model, which gave it the foundations it needed to embark on its rapid restaurant rollout in its second decade in China.

Another critical factor was the decision to appoint Sam Su to head up its China operations in the first place. Su quickly surrounded himself with a new senior team. Like Su himself, most of them had been raised in Taiwan, had experience doing business in international settings, and understood the nuances of working in a Chinese business environment. With this team in place, KFC set out to develop a business that was sensitive to the customs and habits of Chinese consumers. This is of vital importance when dealing with such a culturally sensitive product as food. It was only possible because Su and his team operated with a deep, ingrained awareness of the nuances of the China market and work environment.

Putting in place a team that understands China's complexities is of vital importance. That doesn't mean that all team members have to be Chinese. Indeed, companies can create problems by putting someone in place simply because she or he has a certain ethnic background. But it does mean that companies should think long and hard before staffing a key post with someone with a strong business background but little China experience. It also suggests that rotating people in and out of the country may be the wrong approach to talent management: in-country experience is extremely valuable and worth keeping focused on China.

A related third factor was the fit with China: KFC deliberately adopted products and practices that would mesh well with the inherent qualities of the Chinese markets it was trying to reach. Far too many companies start with the false perception of China as an undeveloped but fast-growing market; they conclude that products and systems that have proved successful elsewhere should have a high chance of succeeding in China. That premise puts their thinking into a box from which it can be hard to escape.

Fourth, KFC put all of its employees' knowledge to work. Su's team chose the right people to take care of its business, and then let them do things as they saw best in the light of local conditions. They avoided bringing in practices from elsewhere until they had been tested and found to work. Inside the restaurants, they trained staff: one manager who worked for Su says it takes five years for a local manager to develop an in-depth understanding of how to manage a Western-style fast-food restaurant. Outside, they worked with suppliers and built out a dedicated, in-house logistics and distribution network—city by city, region by region.

A final factor was patience. The members of Su's senior team took their time. They began by looking at the whole range of the company's operations, from its menu offerings to its supply chain. Their first conclusion: that food, not systems, was the most important thing to get right. They gradually extended the menu, experimenting with different items, often making them available for just a limited period. They invested in ovens so they could offer more than fried food, and began selling juices, salads, and congee, a Chinese version of porridge made from rice. They allowed the extra time they felt was necessary for their strategy, rather than rushing ahead with ambitious expansion plans and hoping for the best.

KFC took nearly a decade to open its first one hundred restaurants. But its patience paid off, with exponentially greater growth in the chain's second decade, and with it the revenues and profits that companies dream of when they think of China.

Companies will always be under enormous pressure to have ambitious short-term growth targets. But the experience of successful and durable companies in China—including IBM and Nokia as well as P&G and KFC—suggests it is better to build slowly and fit practices to China's conditions than to try to work on too many fronts at once, especially if expediency would lead to adopting practices transplanted from outside without carefully assessing their merit. Companies with a longer-range perspective and a solid foundation in China will be much better prospects for both employees and investors.

4. Consumer Culture

As I noted at the start of this chapter, Chinese consumers can choose from an enormous variety of brands and products, possibly more than in any other market worldwide. But while large consumer markets can be found in China's glittering new cities, it would be a mistake to treat them as single homogenized markets. Although China's markets are global in nature, they are also extraordinarily local, rooted in traditional customs and tastes, with extreme variations from one region to the next. In a country with the area and population of China, this should not be surprising.

Even along the coast, the differences among regions is enormous. Shanghai, Zhejiang, Fujian, and Guangdong each have their own spoken dialects (in Guangdong's case, more than one). The Mandarin language unites the northern half of China, but only barely, with major differences in dialects among provinces, and sometimes among neighboring cities. People from Beijing and Shanghai can be easily identified by their speech. Regional tastes remain as strong as ever, especially when it comes to food.

Even in the wealthiest provinces, such as Guangdong, just to the north of Hong Kong, or Zhejiang, to the south of Shanghai, you need only travel a short distance inland and incomes fall abruptly. The rural-urban divide is one that splits the nation, but it is only one of many divides. There is the east coast and the rest of China, especially the far west. Another divide exists between the dry north and the wet south—a disparity that is likely to grow if global warming proceeds as expected later in this century. There is another gap between the densely populated east and center of the country, and the sparse west and northwest. Within cities, there is a divide between permanent residents and migrant workers lured from inland provinces.

The combination of fast but differing rates of growth, population movement, and continual economic and business restructuring, all taking place across a continent-sized country, means that China and its markets are both diverse and complicated in multiple dimensions. Although development is making China more homogeneous in some ways—electricity, television, and roads penetrate even the most remote areas—in others it is becoming less so. Mass media, the Internet, and overseas channels are opening up segments of the population to influences from outside the country. Young people are forming their own interests, distinct from those of their parents and older generations.

With all this come big differences in levels of exposure to and knowledge of products and services—and major variations among the markets that companies are trying to capture. The speed with which China has developed has disrupted traditional patterns of consumer development that build brand loyalty over time. In China, instead of products arriving in a predetermined order, from essentials to luxuries, from low end to high, everything has arrived almost simultaneously. People who were living in frugal, company-assigned and -owned apartments a decade ago now have their own homes, a huge array of consumer durables, access to a raft of brands for every daily purchase, and (in many cases) cars. With little or no history of consumption, these consumers are hard to reach with conventional marketing techniques developed elsewhere. Thus the masses of Chinese people tend to be difficult for marketers to reach: fickle, willing to change brands rapidly, often shopping on price alone. And yet there is a rapidly growing group of people at the high end, who are very brand conscious, with the ultimate goal of showing off their wealth as they acquire known brand products. With markets and tastes continuing to change rapidly, it is difficult to predict what kind of evolutionary path China's consumers will follow.

Will the evolution of the Chinese market continue to be different from elsewhere? Over time consumer habits and tastes may converge with those in other markets, but perhaps only to a degree, and it will take some time. For the next decade, many differences and variations will distinguish the Chinese market from the rest of the world. China remains open to entry, but before they enter, most companies should focus on developing an awareness of Chinese cultural ways and patterns, and how these are changing under the nation's new openness. In addition, any company intent on penetrating China's markets will have to take a clear look at its competitors. Just as China's openness has allowed foreign companies to enter the market, it has also bred one of the fiercest competitive environments in the world, the topic of the next chapter.

CHAPTER 3

Entrepreneurial China

Huawei Technologies represents a prime example of China's entrepreneurial power. The company was founded in 1988 to import and sell office switchboards, and started making the digital switches used to connect telephone calls soon thereafter. In the 1990s, it rode China's telecommunications boom, expanding its product lines to supply the country's fixed-line and mobile-phone companies and quickly becoming a well-established domestic telecommunications business. By the early 2000s, Huawei had annual revenues of around $2 billion—a hugely impressive performance, almost completely derived from its domestic Chinese business.

When the Internet bubble burst in 2000, Huawei's founder and chairman, a former Chinese army officer named Ren Zhengfei, anticipated that his industry would slow down. He predicted that his company would face a "winter" of diminished revenues. He may have been right about the industry, but he couldn't have been more wrong about his company. Since the early 2000s, Huawei has transformed itself from a domestic company into a global enterprise selling state-of-the-art equipment to telecom customers in almost every part of the world. In the six years starting in 2003, sales rose more than eightfold, reaching $17 billion; international sales, which were negligible in 2000, accounted for more than three-quarters of annual revenue in 2008.

Today, Huawei is the world's third-largest maker of mobile-infrastructure equipment and the fifth-largest telecom equipment maker overall, just behind Cisco, Ericsson, Nokia Siemens Networks, and Lucent-Alcatel. It played a major role in forcing a global industry restructuring, in which Siemens and Nokia merged their network infrastructure divisions, and Alcatel acquired Lucent. And while its four largest competitors are struggling with the global recession, Huawei's continued growth is evident: China is in the midst of a $40-billion rollout of third-generation mobile networks that will continue at least through 2010.

Huawei's success can be partly attributed to good timing: its establishment in the late 1980s coincided with the first wave of liberalization in China's telecommunications equipment-making sector, which was undertaken to attract foreign investment and technology. But Huawei also encapsulates many of the distinctive features of China's most successful companies. With its speed, aggression, flexibility, and emphasis on growth, it exemplifies the entrepreneurship that was released with the introduction of economic reform in China. Huawei has pushed to the limit its advantages, notably the openness of its home economy, its access to low-cost manufacturing, and the huge domestic demand for communications. It has built on the connections of its powerful CEO within China's government and in the world at large, and it has fed off the government's massive investment in telecommunications infrastructure. Huawei has absorbed the know-how, technologies, and practices brought into China by other companies, applied them to its own product development, and taken those products out to the rest of the world. Huawei's critics may question the extent of Huawei's innovation, or the degree to which it has relied on imitating IBM and other multinationals. But it is undeniable that Huawei has built a successful international business in a very competitive industry.

Huawei remains privately held. It is owned by its employees, it says, although its exact ownership structure, including the size of Ren's stake, remains a closely guarded secret. At the same time, it continues to receive strong state support, particularly in the financing of overseas sales, on the grounds that it is a key player in China's efforts to pull itself up the technology ladder.

One core reason for Huawei's success is the ultracompetitive pricing of its products, made possible by China's low manufacturing costs and government support. But there is far more to its success than low prices. Huawei has extended its value chain to R&D centers around the world—in Dallas and Silicon Valley, Bangalore, Moscow, and Stockholm—and set up joint ventures and partnerships with global companies, including Symantec and Siemens. More than half of its 60,000 employees work in R&D, on which it spends approximately 10 percent of annual revenues. The company has also invested heavily in marketing and other "soft" efforts to raise its profile, including print advertising campaigns in *BusinessWeek* and the *Economist,* and a logo redesign by the global marketing consultancy Interbrand.

The company has had setbacks. Though increasingly successful in Europe, its efforts to penetrate the U.S. market have yet to pay off. Its involvement with the private equity firm Bain Capital in an attempted buyout of the pioneering data transmission technology company 3Com was abandoned after U.S. politicians raised security concerns. And its cost advantages are eroding as competitors find low-cost manufacturing options of their own.

Nonetheless, Huawei is a noteworthy harbinger of China's competitive future. It is one of a handful of Chinese companies that have made the transition from domestic to global success. And the leaders of other Chinese companies are both watching its progress closely and beginning to make similar moves.

As Chinese companies become global competitors, more of them, like Huawei, will have a dramatic influence on their industries. Already, they have changed their country's prevailing business proposition. China is no longer exclusively a source of low-cost manufacturing. It is realizing the potential to be far more: a source of global competitors in every aspect of business on the global stage, including R&D, product development, infrastructure development, and marketing. These companies will draw upon China's unique forces of scale and intensity, using the former to provide them with a foundation for exponential growth and the latter to fuel the drive and ambition of both management and employees. They will also take full advantage of the Chinese government's embrace of globalization. They know that the government intends to foster the growth of companies that can become global players. And they aspire to be among those companies.

For these Chinese companies—and for the multinationals that compete against them—the key to success will lie in their ability to negotiate the intensely entrepreneurial business environment that has sprung up in China during the past ten years. This chapter is devoted to exploring that environment, starting with the new level of product market freedom that has been established through the liberalization of restrictions on ownership and production.

Product Market Freedom

Although it is widely understood that China's economic advances stem from its move from tightly controlled markets to far freer ones, the specific nature of that change is less widely appreciated for foreign companies. Commercial freedom in China has progressed in two ways. First, through ownership freedom, or the lowering of government restrictions on foreign ownership of businesses in China. Second, through product market freedom, or the degree to which the production and sale of goods by foreign companies is free from government restriction. Since the introduction of China's economic reforms, industry after industry has been granted greater freedom in both dimensions.

The precise degrees of ownership and product market freedom vary from one industry to the next, and have changed over time (see exhibit 3-1).

EXHIBIT 3-1 China's product market freedom matrix

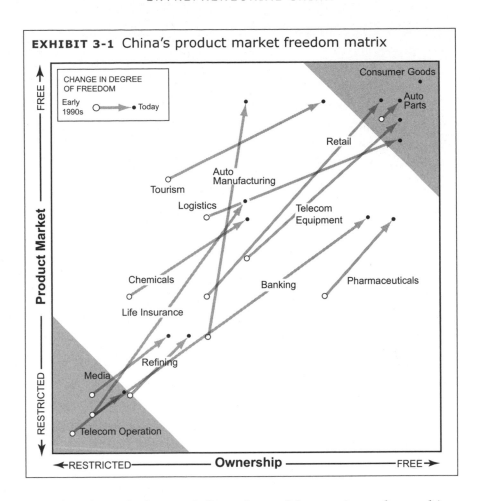

Industries at the bottom left quadrant of the matrix are those subject to the most restrictions. In an economy that was entirely closed to outsiders, almost every industry would be in this corner. Sectors at the top right are the freest and are typical of most industries in a full market economy. In China, starting in the 1980s, but with greater speed since the mid-1990s, the government liberalized industry after industry for foreign participation in the interest of economic growth. As they allowed more foreign participation in more industries, there was a general migration from the bottom left corner toward the upper right.

Some industries have moved further and faster than others. Consumer goods has always been close to the top right-hand corner—high ownership freedom and high product market freedom—because China had decided in the early 1990s that the consumer goods industry was not strategic. Both domestic and foreign companies were allowed a high degree of ownership and operational freedom. Telecommunications operations companies, by contrast, are close to the bottom left. All of China's operators remain majority state-owned, and all of their services are strictly licensed. The number of major operators has increased from one to three, and all of them have secured international stock market listings, but all key decisions, such as a restructuring of the industry in 2008, are made by the government.

Between the extremes of heavily regulated and liberalized industries are those with varying degrees of product market freedom. In some industries, ownership regulations are relatively liberal, but strict controls remain over what kinds of products and services can be offered. In banking, for example, new products are often subjected to long delays before they are approved, and in retailing, gaining permission to open new outlets can be a cumbersome process. In other sectors, ownership freedom is constrained, but there is a high degree of product freedom. No foreign company can own more than 50 percent of a Chinese motor vehicle maker, but there are few constraints on what cars they make or how they sell them.

The issues facing foreign companies and their Chinese competitors vary significantly depending on where their industries are located on the product market freedom matrix. In the more restricted quadrants, companies have to deal with many regulations whose interpretation can vary according to official whim or sentiment. In these industries, often deemed strategic, the government plays a prominent, even dominant, role. Most, if not all, companies operating within them are state owned or controlled. In the less restricted quadrants, foreign companies find themselves facing a proliferation of competitors, often from all corners of the world as well as locally in China, quite likely with a surfeit of productive capacity, and downward pressure on pricing.

For Chinese enterprises, the government's reforms of corporate governance have further encouraged product market freedom. The most important of these reforms, the Company Law of 1994, made it possible for state-owned enterprises (SOEs) to become corporations and their ownership recast in the form of shares. This opened the way for many SOEs to be privatized and either sold outright (often to their managers) or listed on the world's stock exchanges.

Many managers took advantage of the greater autonomy and profits that came with privatization; the Company Law thus led to a massive wave of industrial restructuring in the late 1990s and early 2000s. The importance of profitability was further stressed by tax reforms that changed the previous system, in which companies had shared their profits with the government, to one where they paid taxes to the government but kept the remaining profits for themselves. In a widely heard ultimatum to "perform, or else," the Chinese government made it clear that unprofitable companies could be forced to close. This in fact happened to thousands of companies during this period.

For all their momentum, China's market reforms have been developed piecemeal, with no overall master plan. Official views about the strategic value of each industry have largely shaped the degree to which each sector has been granted ownership and product freedom.

Three Types of Companies

Broadly speaking, the millions of companies operating in China fall into three categories according to their ownership. Publicly owned companies include those owned directly by the national government, by local or city governments, or by neighborhood collectives. The other two categories are privately owned Chinese companies and foreign companies, including enterprises that are wholly owned or jointly owned by non-Chinese owners or investors. Market liberalization has driven a radical shift in the numbers and proportions of these companies (see exhibit 3-2).

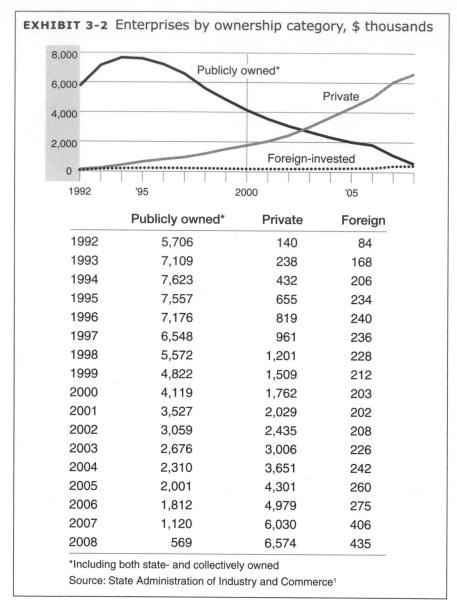

EXHIBIT 3-2 Enterprises by ownership category, $ thousands

	Publicly owned*	Private	Foreign
1992	5,706	140	84
1993	7,109	238	168
1994	7,623	432	206
1995	7,557	655	234
1996	7,176	819	240
1997	6,548	961	236
1998	5,572	1,201	228
1999	4,822	1,509	212
2000	4,119	1,762	203
2001	3,527	2,029	202
2002	3,059	2,435	208
2003	2,676	3,006	226
2004	2,310	3,651	242
2005	2,001	4,301	260
2006	1,812	4,979	275
2007	1,120	6,030	406
2008	569	6,574	435

*Including both state- and collectively owned
Source: State Administration of Industry and Commerce[1]

While the overall number of companies in China has changed surprisingly little in the last fifteen years, the number of publicly owned enterprises, after rising slightly in the early 1990s, has fallen dramatically, from a peak of more than 7.6 million in 1994 to 1.8 million in 2006, and fewer still in the years since. In their place have risen private companies,

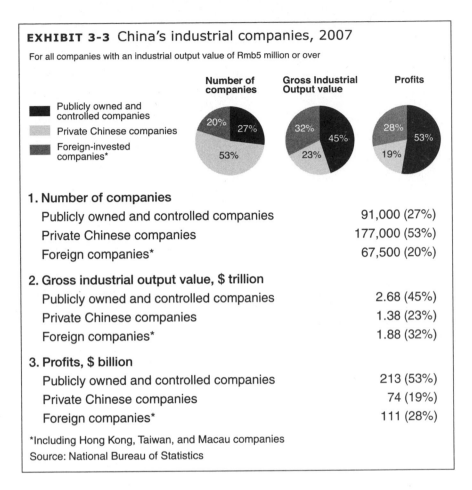

EXHIBIT 3-3 China's industrial companies, 2007

For all companies with an industrial output value of Rmb5 million or over

	Number of companies	Gross Industrial Output value	Profits
Publicly owned and controlled companies			
Private Chinese companies			
Foreign-invested companies*			

Number of companies: 20% / 27% / 53%

Gross Industrial Output value: 32% / 45% / 23%

Profits: 28% / 53% / 19%

1. Number of companies

Publicly owned and controlled companies	91,000 (27%)
Private Chinese companies	177,000 (53%)
Foreign companies*	67,500 (20%)

2. Gross industrial output value, $ trillion

Publicly owned and controlled companies	2.68 (45%)
Private Chinese companies	1.38 (23%)
Foreign companies*	1.88 (32%)

3. Profits, $ billion

Publicly owned and controlled companies	213 (53%)
Private Chinese companies	74 (19%)
Foreign companies*	111 (28%)

*Including Hong Kong, Taiwan, and Macau companies
Source: National Bureau of Statistics

which have increased from just 140,000 in 1992 to almost 5 million in 2006, and to a lesser extent, foreign companies, whose numbers have trebled from less than 100,000 to around 300,000 in the same period.

The shrinking number of public companies, however, should not be mistaken as a sign of the eventual demise of the state sector. In fact, they remain the core of the Chinese economy. Publicly owned companies account for just over one-quarter of the total companies, but, as seen in exhibit 3-3, they produce 45 percent of China's industrial value and more than half of industrial profits.

Nor does the relatively small number of foreign companies mean that they are unimportant. They produce nearly 60 percent of China's exports, account for one-fifth of all industrial companies, and produce nearly one-third of industrial output, although they are less profitable than the state companies.

Private companies, though far more numerous than both publicly owned and foreign companies combined, produce far less output and profit. They make less than one-quarter of China's industrial output and less than one-fifth of total profits.

Anyone trying to make sense of China's business landscape will need to understand the strategic agendas driving each of the three types of companies, along with their strengths, the pressures they are subjected to, and the kinds of responses they are likely to make to these conditions.

1. Publicly Owned Companies

For leaders of global corporations trying to develop a sound China strategy, the vast majority of the country's publicly owned companies are of little significance. More than 1 million of them are neighborhood collectives, owned by the local people who work in them. Almost all of the rest, numbering about 700,000, are owned by city or provincial governments and provide jobs and support for their local economies. These businesses are remnants of China's socialist era, and many will either disappear or be converted into private enterprises during the next ten years.

The national government, however, has retained control over a tiny but enormously powerful group of businesses. These number around 150 companies, of which 50 form an inner core. They include all of the country's largest companies; as shown in exhibit 3-4, every one of China's top twenty companies by revenue are state-owned enterprises.

China's largest SOEs almost all lie in the most closed and regulated sectors of the economy, the bottom left quadrant of the product mar-

EXHIBIT 3-4 Chinese companies in *Fortune*'s Global 500, 2008
Revenues (in millions of U.S. dollars)

1. China Petroleum & Chemical Corp. (Sinopec)	$207.8
2. China National Petroleum Corp. (PetroChina)	181.1
3. State Grid	164.1
4. Industrial & Commercial Bank of China	70.6
5. China Mobile Communications	65.0
6. China Construction Bank	58.0
7. China Life Insurance	54.5
8. Bank of China	51.3
9. Agricultural Bank of China	48.1
10. Sinochem	44.5
11. China Southern Power Grid	41.1
12. Baosteel Group	35.5
13. China Railway Group	33.8
14. China Railway Construction	32.5
15. China Telecom	31.8
16. China State Construction Engineering	29.8
17. China National Offshore Oil	38.0
18. China Ocean Shipping Company (COSCO)	27.4
19. China Minmetals	26.7
20. China National Cereals, Oils & Foodstuffs Corp. (COFCO)	26.4
21. China Communications Construction	26.0
22. Shanghai Automotive Industry Corp.	24.9
23. Sinosteel	24.2
24. Hebei Iron & Steel Group	24.0
25. China Metallurgical Group	23.8
26. China FAW Group	23.7
27. Citic Group	22.2
28. China United Telecommunications	22.0
29. China Huaneng Group	21.8
30. Aviation Industry Corp. of China	21.7
31. China South Industries Group	21.7
32. Jiangsu Shagang Group	21.0
33. Bank of Communications	18.7
34. Aluminium Corp. of China	18.6

Source: *Fortune*[2]

ket freedom matrix. They all operate in industries that the government deems strategic, and competition between them is closely managed. For example, the telecommunications services industry is divided between three state-owned companies: China Telecom, China Mobile, and China Unicom. The oil and gas industry is dominated by

three state-owned companies: China Petroleum and Chemical Corporation (usually referred to as Sinopec); China National Petroleum Corporation (CNPC, or better known through its listed arm, PetroChina);
and China National Offshore Oil Corporation (CNOOC). Other industries dominated by state-owned giants include automobile manufacturing, power transmission, construction, transportation, steel,
and metallurgy.

Ownership of almost all these businesses is vested in a central government holding company, the state-owned Assets Supervision and
Administration Commission (SASAC). The only significant exceptions
are the major banks, whose ownership is vested with the Ministry of
Finance. SASAC has devised an elaborate series of management controls for the companies under its oversight, with performance contracts
and considerable pressure on their managers to produce both growth
and profits.

Because of the limited amount of competition allowed in the industries in which they operate, these SOEs are large and profitable.
While some of them have raised money through the world's stock
markets, only small stakes, usually between 10 percent and 25 percent,
have been sold, and in no instance has management control been
ceded. Sino-foreign joint ventures have been allowed in SOEs, but always with caps on foreign ownership, such as the 50 percent limit in
the automotive industry.

These companies are likely to remain leaders in their domestic industries—the markets for energy, resources, telecom services, and the
rest are certain to remain protected—but even being invested in or
having a joint venture with a major Chinese company is unlikely to
offer foreign companies any guarantees of long-term access to China.
In the automotive industry, for example, although the global carmakers now dominate the sector through their joint ventures with the large
Chinese automotive firms, the government has repeatedly made it
clear that it ultimately plans to establish a handful of strong domestic
companies.

China's powerful SOEs, particularly those in energy and commodities, are also among its most globally active companies. They have the financial resources necessary to pursue even the largest of deals, and a government mandate to secure the resources China needs to maintain its economic growth. This government support makes them ever more formidable competitors in global markets.

The biggest challenge these companies have encountered thus far is political resistance from foreign nations suspicious of their motives and their government ties. This was evident in 2005, when CNOOC's bid for the American oil company Unocal was thwarted by political opposition in the United States. Similar resistance was the key reason for the failure of the Bain Capital–Huawei buyout of 3Com. And it was the main reason behind the Australian government's long and close scrutiny of the proposed investment of $19.5 billion by China's principal aluminum producer, the Aluminum Corporation of China (Chinalco), in the Anglo-Australian mining company Rio Tinto in 2009; the deal was ultimately rejected by Rio Tinto's board.

2. Private Sector Companies

Practically nonexistent at the start of the 1990s, private sector companies have become a significant and growing part of China's economy. (I use the term *private companies* here to refer to all companies with primarily nongovernmental owners, including both those listed and unlisted on public stock exchanges.) The number of Chinese who are either self-employed or working in private companies has risen from around 8 million in 1992 to nearly 80 million in 2008. The private companies' share of China's total industrial output and profits may be low now, but most are still young and the competition in the sectors in which they are free to operate is far greater than in the protected industries where SOEs hold sway. But as the private sector continues to mature, the opportunities for entrepreneurial companies will increase.

The vast majority of new Chinese companies fall into this category. They are highly competitive and very dynamic. They have adopted market-driven mechanisms and outlooks, are extremely fast to react and willing to experiment, and are driven by ambition and a belief that they have at least as much right to succeed as anyone else. Many of these companies are already well known within China and have the potential to become influential forces in their global industries. Their ranks include almost all of China's "fast" companies, among them technology firms, such as Baidu, China's leading Internet search company, QQ, China's hugely successful Internet messaging company, and the business-to-business e-commerce portal Alibaba.com; manufacturers, such as the home appliances firm Midea and automotive components maker Wanxiang; and retailers, such as the electronics chain GOME and appliance retailer Suning.

Mindray, a leading developer, manufacturer, and marketer of medical devices (such as patient monitoring devices, in-vitro diagnostic instruments, biochemistry analyzers, and medical imaging systems), is a noteworthy example of a successful new entrepreneurial company. It started in 1991 with a three-person team; by 2009 it had 5,600 employees, introduced six to eight new products per year, and claimed nearly twenty "China's firsts" among its portfolio of products. Mindray's leaders attribute their success to a deep-rooted commitment to continuously invest in R&D and to continuously push for innovation. Over the years, regardless of the company's ups and downs, they have never wavered from these beliefs; this has allowed them to build a globally competitive business based on Chinese human resources.

Another example is Dongxiang, a rapidly growing multibrand sportswear company that owns the exclusive rights to Italy's Kappa brand in China and Macau. Started only seven years ago, Dongxiang is now among the top five companies in China's sportswear sector in market share. The others are Nike, Adidas, Li Ning, and Anta. Like Adidas and Nike, Dongxiang outsources all its manufacturing. However, while the company's revenue is only about one-quarter of Nike's in China, its operating margin in 2008 was 42 percent: far higher than the 10 to 15 percent of its key competitors. Dongxiang's performance can be attributed to its focus on a market sector that was previously ignored: sports-loving, fashion-conscious eighteen- to thirty-five-year-olds. Targeting this segment allowed it to increase its retail prices with a 7 to 10 percent premium over similar products from its competitors.

Dongxiang has also leveraged Kappa's international marketing strategies while it developed its own innovative marketing practices as well. These have brought its advertising and promotion costs down to less than half those of its international competitors. During soccer's 2006 World Cup, Li Ning spent Rmb 30 million (about $3.75 million) advertising on China's main television channels, and Adidas invested ten times that amount or more on China's national team, which failed to make it past the competition's first round. Dongxiang spent less than Rmb 2 million (about $250,000) on sponsorship, concentrating on sending a team of Chinese entertainment celebrities to Germany. Dressed in Kappa apparel, these celebrities attracted the attention of many Chinese reporters and their activities were widely reported in print, broadcast, and online media.

Private companies are concentrated in China's least regulated, most fragmented economic sectors. They receive correspondingly little official support (even securing bank loans can be difficult), but this has made them very resourceful. To date, their main focus has been China's domestic markets. Many of the sectors they operate in are fragmented and ready for consolidation, although it is still not clear when any substantial number of mergers and acquisitions will happen.

Some of these businesses, such as Huawei, are privately owned but behave in many ways as if they were state-owned enterprises. Others are publicly held but act like private companies, such as Haier, the world's fourth-largest maker of white goods, which officially remains classified as a collective. There are three major reasons for understanding private companies and taking their influence seriously: their fast growth rates, the kind of innovations they are making, and the changes they are making in global value chains.

3. Foreign Companies

In the economic development of China, the role of companies that are foreign-owned, or largely owned by non-Chinese investors, should not be underestimated. These companies have brought capital, technologies, expertise, and—most valuable of all—exposure to managerial practices from around the world. As we saw in chapter 2, their importance to the Chinese economy, as exporters and producers, has been directly linked to the government's openness.

Foreign companies generally occupy the same quadrants on the product market freedom matrix as the Chinese private companies they compete against, but in many ways, they remain distinctly separate. Whereas many private Chinese companies concentrate on producing and selling less expensive goods in the lower tiers of their markets, and some are beginning to develop medium- to high-end products in higher-tier markets, the foreign companies tend to concentrate their efforts solely at the high end. Foreign and nonmainland companies, especially those from Hong Kong and Taiwan, also tend to be externally oriented, hence the large share of exports from this group. (The Chinese government considers companies from Hong Kong and Taiwan "foreign" from the standpoint of investment regulations and corporate identity.)

In terms of their impact on China's business environment, the most important foreign companies are the large multinationals that have arrived from America, Europe, Japan, and other countries to manufacture and source goods for sale elsewhere or to sell to China's markets. Some are resource companies, such as BHP Billiton and Rio Tinto from Australia and Vale from Brazil, which supply metals and other raw materials to the Chinese manufacturing sectors. Other foreign companies have played a key role in shaping the competitive landscape in a host of major industries—automotive, chemicals, consumer goods, electronics, financial services, information technology, logistics, pharmaceuticals, and retailing among them.

However, nowhere have foreign companies had the field to themselves. Wherever they have entered, Chinese companies have sprung up to compete against them. And though foreign companies will continue to play a major role in the Chinese economy, they are certain to see their currently high shares of industrial output and exports drop over time.

Until now, most outside companies have concentrated on either low-cost manufacturing for export or on production for marketing within China. Relatively few arrived with plans for integrated operations, seeking to combine both. In the automotive industry, for example, of all the Sino-foreign joint ventures established, only Honda and Shanghai GM export cars; every other company is focused on developing their market within China. One major story of the next decade, and of this book, is the coming change in this dynamic as companies are forced to produce and market in China for both domestic and foreign customers.

The Context of Investment

All three company ownership categories have ridden an enormous wave of investment in China during the past fifteen years. The flow of foreign capital, which is approaching $1 trillion since the start of economic reforms, also brought with it new products and technologies, expertise, and practices.[3] But even this surge in foreign capital has been overshadowed by the volume of investment from Chinese sources—from the government at all levels, in spending on infrastructure, and from Chinese companies, both public and private, investing and reinvesting in productive capacity.

This domestic investment has been the most significant underreported factor in the growth of China's manufacturing sector, particularly that spent on infrastructure. Its overall level of investment is unprecedented, not just in China, but anywhere. And it started well before the "stimulus" package of late 2008. Since the early 1990s, gross capital formation—the share of money invested in capital assets such as buildings, roads, machinery, and equipment—has been approximately 35 percent of gross domestic product, rising to 40 percent in the early to mid-2000s. Other countries, including Japan and South Korea, approached China's investment rate, but in each case only for a handful of years. Not one of them maintained the same sustained level of spending for so many years.

The most spectacular results can be found in China's industrial development zones. Many of these amount to satellite cities in their own right, with populations of several hundred thousand, their own universities, convention and exhibition centers, hotels, and leisure facilities such as golf courses, parks, and lakes. These zones cost billions of dollars to build, but, in turn, they have attracted tens of billions of dollars of capital from multinational companies.

China's domestic companies, both publicly owned and private, have strong incentives to keep investing and reinvesting. Few companies see returning dividends to their shareholders as important, preferring to expand their productive capacity. Publicly owned companies, especially at a local level, invest to create jobs and boost their local economies. Pride also plays a part, with every province seeking a full range of industries, from automotive to information technology. This ambition has led to both a surge in capacity in just about every industry and the heated competition that has come to characterize the liberalized markets in the Chinese economy.

It has also led to charges of waste. China is often criticized for spending lots of money inefficiently: building unneeded commercial towers and government offices, bridges that have little traffic, and factories in industries that already have large amounts of excess capacity. But such criticisms overlook the overall effect of the investment boom: it created China's industrial infrastructure, and it will drive the next phase of economic development.

To date, most investment has gone to establishing the basic requirements of industrial society: roads, ports, and power stations, telecommunications networks, factories, and equipment. This work is far from finished and is a major part of the government's stimulus measures introduced to keep the economy growing strongly through the global economic slowdown. As such, much of the force behind China's growth has been extensive—adding more infrastructure—rather than intensive—getting more out of existing facilities.

There are, of course, limits to just how long such expansion can continue. Ultimately, China will have to shift from an investment-driven model of growth to a demand-driven model in which private consumption plays the greater role. And along the way, companies, particularly domestic ones, will have to shift their emphasis from producing more in whatever way possible to increasing productivity: realizing more value from the same amount of inputs.

The strong demand created by China's fast growth has allowed many companies to postpone this reckoning—until now. The weaker demand generated by the global economic slowdown, however, has forced many companies to look more closely at their productivity. Broadly speaking, Chinese and foreign companies are going about this in different ways. Foreign companies are looking at ways in which they can expand their activities in China by increasing the range of tasks they do in China through a process of *value-chain migration*. Chinese companies, for a variety of reasons, are largely focused on strengthening their existing operations, in particular by looking for innovative and more efficient means to produce goods.

The rest of this chapter explores these two responses and how they are creating the foundation for a shift from China's expansive development to a more intensive kind of development: the search for new ways to enhance the value generated within China's economy.

The Foreign Response: Value-Chain Migration

Value-chain migration refers to the geographic relocation of portions of a company's supply, distribution, and value creation activity. It usually begins with a straightforward and discrete process, such as manufacturing.

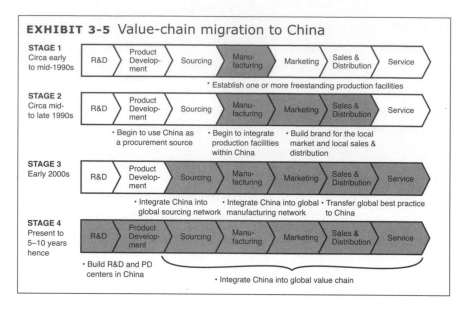

EXHIBIT 3-5 Value-chain migration to China

Then other functions follow. For many multinationals, this process has involved moving some parts of their business to different locations around the world; rarely, however, have they moved entire value chains from one location to another.

In the past two decades, globalization has led to both an increase in and an acceleration of value-chain migration, with companies moving more of their functions—call centers and back-office services to India, manufacturing to Mexico, or research to centers of excellence in Israel and Russia. China, of course, has become a primary production location for a large share of the world's manufactured goods.

But other functions besides manufacturing have also shifted to China, seeking to take advantage of China's indigenous strengths in other areas, such as scientific research. This migration has gone through four stages over the past two decades (see exhibit 3-5).

The first stage, the migration of simple manufacturing, started in the late 1980s and gained momentum from the mid-1990s onward. Companies set up production facilities, typically on a one-off basis to manufacture or assemble export goods and, less frequently, to test China's domestic markets. For example, all of the world's consumer electronics firms—Japanese, European, and American—set up factories to assemble their products along the Chinese coast.

In the second stage, starting in the mid- to late 1990s, China became a major sourcing location as more and more suppliers arrived, leading to the establishment of reliable production networks. As these networks evolved, some companies began to integrate their production facilities within China, while others set about establishing their brands and building domestic sales and distribution networks. The electronics companies that previously had put together their goods from imported parts were increasingly able to use locally manufactured components, made either by other multinationals, particularly those from Taiwan, or, increasingly, from Chinese companies setting themselves up in competition with such companies.

In the third stage, starting during the early 2000s and continuing today, companies began to integrate China into their global sourcing and manufacturing networks and transfer their global best practices to the country. Some companies established research and development operations in China as part of their global R&D functions, but these were mainly focused on product development rather than basic research. Others that had been selling imported high-end goods into the country, such as the automakers BMW and Mercedes-Benz, established more complex manufacturing operations that could in turn be used to supply their factories in other parts of the world. At the same time, marketing and sales operations increased in scale and sophistication. Although still constrained by distribution shortcomings, more companies built networks capable of reaching China's most prosperous regions and started planning how to reach its second-, third-, and fourth-tier cities.

The final stage, which has already started for a handful of companies but will be one of the main features of the next decade, will see companies make their China operations a totally integrated part of their global value chains. No longer will their businesses in the country be seen as freestanding elements. Instead, they will become a major source of value for a business's operations in other parts of the world, leading to the creation of one world companies. (Chapter 5 of this book explores the nature of these businesses in depth.)

Such companies will strive to make China the source of new products for both its own markets and the rest of the world; their operations in the country will also act as a conduit through which goods developed elsewhere can be marketed and sold in China. They will tap into the functions at which China excels—among them research for many manufacturing and high-technology industries and supply-chain management skills related to manufacturing—to develop new goods and move them to the rest of the world in the most efficient manner possible. Among the few companies that have already started down this path are Nokia, which has succeeded in leveraging the growth of China's mobile-phone user base to make the country both its leading production center and a primary source of new phone developments, and IBM, which has located one of its global R&D laboratories and its worldwide procurement headquarters in China (IBM's strategy is described in detail in chapter 5).

Of course, not every company will follow this sequence as neatly as depicted. However, the importance of value chain migration in corporate China is clear. Already it has played a critical role in moving China from being a manufacturing or sourcing location to offering a diverse range of business advantages. Because of the speed with which this change has occurred, most companies have yet to grasp just how extensive these advantages are and what potential they may offer—though they will soon.

The Chinese Response: New Ways of Innovation

Value-chain migration has principally been a process involving foreign multinationals, but it has its counterpart in Chinese companies searching for new ways to strengthen their competitive positions. The leaders of most of these companies believe that innovative products and processes lie at the heart of long-term corporate success. This view is shared by Chinese government officials; the government has explicitly stated that its long-term objective is the development of a knowledge-driven economy that in large part draws its strength from homegrown technologies. China's current five-year plan—its eleventh such plan, which covers the period from 2006 to 2010—identifies the promotion of technological innovation to increase value and develop a sustainable economy as a top priority.

The government is driving technological advances in a variety of domains. These include an ambitious space program: China launched its first manned spacecraft, *Shenzhou V*, in 2003 and has plans to go to the moon and beyond. There are also government initiatives in aerospace and railroad research and development. In 2005, the world's highest railway was completed, traveling a route from Xining in Qinghai province to Lhasa, the Tibetan capital. About 600 miles runs 13,000 or more feet above sea level. The government has also unveiled plans for a new commercial short- to medium-range airplane. The C919 is scheduled to take its maiden voyage in 2014 and will start delivery to buyers in 2016. The project represents a major first step by China toward developing a homegrown commercial aircraft manufacturing industry that will develop planes for its fast-growing domestic market—and that could ultimately enter into head-to-head competition with Western rivals like Boeing and Airbus.

Chinese companies will seek to strengthen themselves, like Japanese and South Korean companies before them, by gradually abandoning their emphasis on making low-cost, low-end goods to making more expensive, value-laden goods. To achieve this, Chinese companies will make goods that are more advanced, contain new technologies, draw on the strength of an established brand name, and so on. In short, they will become more like the multinationals from America, Europe, and Japan, but probably with an unprecedented speed of activity.

To some extent, this is happening already, especially among the largest Chinese companies. Huawei, for example, is following the footsteps of established high-technology companies, such as Cisco Systems, in its brand-building efforts. It has also invested heavily in improving its management prowess, working with Western consulting firms, and recruiting managerial talent from Western business schools. Other examples include Himin Group, the world's largest manufacturing base of solar thermal products; Suntech, another leading global solar energy company; and Goldwind Science and Technology Company, the market leader in wind turbine power generation in China and the eighth largest in worldwide revenues.

But although the desired path forward is obvious to most Chinese leaders, there are barriers. For those domestic companies that operate on thin margins, where will they find the funds to invest in R&D? The protection of their investments in innovation is another problem; foreign companies complain loudly about intellectual property piracy, but domestic companies are also vulnerable to the loss of proprietary knowledge. Huawei chairman Ren Zhengfei has been very vocal about the potential negative impact of China's lack of intellectual property protection on domestic technology companies, including his own company. And what about talent? Given the fact that multinationals with deep pockets struggle to find experienced employees, how will Chinese companies find the talented people needed to upgrade and transform their operations?

While it is widely accepted that fostering a culture of innovation is a must, many Chinese businesspeople have not fully grasped what this entails. A case in point: When I met with managers at one of the leading industrial SOEs, they were interested in learning how to improve their innovation capabilities. However, they were equally, if not more, interested in understanding how innovation could be measured. The reason for this is that the government evaluated performance with a scorecard for each manager. Their staff would only have an incentive to focus attention on innovation if a section for it was incorporated into the scorecard. Looking good on the numbers was more important to the people of this company than any real innovation results.

Nonetheless, there are more and more examples of this genuine capability among Chinese companies. One particularly innovative domain has been in specific portions of the value chain. As Ming Zeng, a former professor at the Cheung Kong Graduate School of Business in Beijing and chief strategy officer at Alibaba.com, and Peter Williamson, a professor at Europe's INSEAD business school, point out in their book, *Dragons at Your Door: How Chinese Cost Innovation Is Disrupting Global Competition*,[4] the modularization of many products and the outsourcing of these modules has been a major source of competitiveness for Chinese companies. By bringing the strengths of the Chinese manufacturing model to bear on one or two product lines, companies can produce particular components or subassemblies more cheaply and in greater volume than before. Although its name may not appear on the final product, its very entry can disrupt an existing configuration of suppliers. Wanxiang Group, for example, began its growth to become one of China's leading automotive components producers by concentrating on making itself the dominant force in universal joints.

Another form of innovation being undertaken by Chinese companies is more controversial, especially outside of China. It involves the production of low-cost *shan zhai* goods. Originally, *shan zhai* was used to refer to a bandit stronghold outside government control; today it is shorthand for a multitude of knockoffs, fakes, and pirated products. These include everything from mobile phones to medicine and movies to makeup, and they permeate China's consumer markets.

Many observers write off the producers of such goods as nothing more than counterfeiters or pirates, but they are worth studying—not just because of the competitive threat they pose, but for their legitimate impact on business. The best *shan zhai* firms, which have established themselves not through thievery but through knockoffs and imitations, have also disrupted the status quo by inventing new and ingenious business strategies tailored specifically to local markets.

By expanding the range of available products, especially at lower price points, *shan zhai* companies grow markets by making them more accessible to low-income consumers. They also stimulate competition by disrupting the hegemony of established players, and they encourage grassroots innovation at home. They often target less developed areas such as lower-tier cities and the countryside. Although individual incomes in these markets are lower, aggregate consumer purchasing power can still be significant, especially since younger, rural consumers tend to watch and adopt urban consumption trends.

Future Cola, once labeled a cheap copycat of Coca-Cola, is a good example. Now the third-largest player in China's carbonated soft drinks market, right after Pepsi, Future Cola's first product copied Coca-Cola's packaging design, but its flavor was tailored to the Chinese palette. Unlike Coca-Cola, which targeted major cities, Future Cola sought out overlooked consumers in rural areas. It imported state-of-the-art equipment and quickly localized production facilities, allowing it to offer products at significantly lower price points. It also launched an aggressive, highly focused marketing campaign aimed at building a brand image as "The Chinese People's Own Cola."

Similarly, the mobile-phone maker Tianyu started off by focusing on previously neglected low-end handset users in third- and fourth-tier cities, aggressively rolling out a channel strategy overlooked by majors, such as Motorola and Nokia, which targeted "last-mile" sales. This involved development of a streamlined distribution model that offered products mainly at points of sale in retail chain stores and supermarket electronics counters, and paying generous sales commissions directly to the salespeople working in these locations. Tianyu took just two years to overtake number-one domestic player Lenovo, and is now closing the gap on foreign giants that lead the market: Nokia, Samsung, and Motorola.

The most successful *shan zhai* companies have a few common characteristics:

- They tend to target mass markets, particularly lower-tier ones.
- They have short cycle times for new product introductions.

- They focus on offering the cheapest version of a product, often accepting lower quality as a consequence.
- They tailor product features and functions to local requirements.

The most salient quality of many *shan zhai* companies is their willingness to take chances and learn from their experiences. "Let's try it," they say. If an idea doesn't work, they abandon it and try something else. The most adept *shan zhai* practitioners use their ability to experiment, replicate success, and move rapidly up the learning curve, to outcompete many slower-moving foreign and state-owned competitors.

Of course, there are many *shan zhai* companies that operate in breach of, or at least on the borderline of, China's intellectual property laws. But these cheap copycat-type operators are generally short-lived. Some *shan zhai* companies are evolving into legitimate businesses with their own intellectual property portfolios. And others are becoming nimble mainstream competitors, taking advantage of the often slow and occasionally negligent responsiveness of industry incumbents in reacting to market changes. Established players open the door to such competition when they fail to respond quickly to evolving markets; adapt to changing consumer preferences or have an inadequate understanding of local market dynamics (a common failure among foreign companies); or are persistently reluctant to implement change (a common failure among large Chinese SOEs).

China's car rental industry shows how major foreign companies can be outmaneuvered. Hertz, the world's largest car-rental company, entered China in 2002. But despite having a first-mover advantage and years of industry experience, it was slow to develop its Chinese operations, as was Avis, the number-two global brand. One reason for this was that both companies tried to apply their American operating models, in which Chinese renters would drive the cars themselves. This strategy left the door open for a domestic player, "eHi Car rental," whose leaders recognized that the self-drive approach didn't suit the needs of busy and often stressed local executives, especially in China's heavy traffic and rapidly evolving road systems. eHi offered chauffeur-driven cars, a move that quickly made it the only large car-rental company that is profitable in China.

Shan zhai manufacturers take full advantage of China's production capacity and supply-chain capabilities. Most *shan zhai* mobile phones are developed in Shenzhen. There more than 30,000 companies collaborate across the entire mobile-phone value chain, from designing products through sourcing, and then from assembly and production to testing, packaging, distribution, and after-sales services.

The very best *shan zhai* players are constantly looking for the next opportunity—one that can offer new growth before the markets for their current products come to the end of their life cycles. Tianyu, for example, developed a very responsive operation capable of fast product manufacturing turnarounds. Launching more than a hundred tailored models within a year, it created a wide spectrum of product choice for its channel partners and, ultimately, its customers. The resultant high sales volumes led to rapidly growing market share. Now, the company is investing in 3G products, aiming at the next phase of China's telecom development. Following an agreement with Qualcomm, it will soon be manufacturing and selling a range of handsets compatible with China's upcoming 3G networks. Today, Tianyu is virtually unrecognizable as a *shan zhai* company, becoming a mainstream player thanks largely to increased efforts in R&D and brand building. In the long run, the *shan zhai* approach will be constrained by its own contradictions: China's own increasing home-grown R&D efforts will also be threatened by loose intellectual property practices, so those will inevitably tighten. In the short run, companies in China will compete by making their products difficult to imitate. Honeywell, as we'll see in chapter 6, is one example. Another is Apple; though there are many Chinese iPhone knockoffs, they can never provide the customer service and connections that Apple developed through alliances with local companies. Similarly, Toyota overcame some fake-parts competitors through aggressive pricing and local production facilities.

The Future of Entrepreneurial China

The downside of Chinese entrepreneurship is the vicious cycle of commoditization: its relentless focus on cost reduction heightens the price competition for products and services, which leads to more cost reductions. This has raised questions about the long-term viability of the low-cost strategy. Huawei and China's other telecommunications equipment buyers may be thriving, but some companies in other industries, such as Changhong (a low-cost television-set maker) and most of the country's various mobile handset manufacturers are all high-volume, low-margin producers. They either have found or could find themselves struggling as their industries embrace new technologies. The economic fallout from the global financial crisis and recession will also affect the future of China's companies by weeding out weaker companies, particularly those that depend mainly on recession-hit export markets.

China's stronger companies will most likely emerge leaner, with larger market shares and better positions on their industry value chains. Some will make overseas acquisitions that will enhance their technological assets, marketing reach, and managerial expertise. Among the world's industries where a greater Chinese presence can be expected are automotive components, transport equipment, shipbuilding, mining, machinery, and components for computers and other IT products.

These companies will not stop figuring out ways of producing goods more cheaply; that cost pressure will continue. But they will also figure out ways of producing goods more effectively, applying and reapplying the lessons they have learned. Witness the success of Haier, which has figured out how to sell niche goods in developed markets, and Fuyao Glass, a maker of glass for the automotive industry, which has made itself a supplier to many China-based car producers.

An increasing number of Chinese entrepreneurs recognize the importance of building their own brands and moving up their industry value chains. This phenomenon is most prevalent in hotly contested sectors where there is no or little government protection. In the apparel industry, for instance, Chinese brands such as Metersbonwe, Semir, and Bosideng are leaders. In the sporting goods sector, Li Ning, Dongxiang, Anta, and 361 Degrees are major brands. In the automotive sector, many Chinese manufacturers have pursued their own brand strategies. One example is BYD. Another is the Shanghai Automotive Industry Corporation (SAIC), whose Roewe brand is targeted to the mid- to high-end sectors. Other automotive makers such as Chery, Geely, Great Wall, Changan, Dongfeng, and First Auto Works are all pursuing their own brand strategies.

The net effect will be the creation of a new Chinese business culture. This culture is very different from that of America, Europe, and Japan, or even of Hong Kong, Taiwan, and the overseas Chinese communities of southeast Asia. It is simultaneously developing in two directions: a "Westernized" direction, which is absorbing the management techniques of multinational companies, and a more "Chinese" direction, which draws on the characteristics of the local environments. China's new business culture features these core traits:

1. Bursts of entrepreneurship when opportunities present themselves. The Chinese business culture is highly risk-tolerant. Having risen so far so fast, often making decisions when there is little information to gauge the likely success of a venture, and consequently finding their hunches were accurate, many companies are happy to continue operating in such a rough-and-ready manner.

2. An emphasis on speed. Planning and evaluation have their roles, but they are subordinate to the need for fast decisions and immediate action. This culture doesn't let practices get bogged down in bureaucracy.

3. A preference for imitation and experimentation over innovation, with an emphasis on cycles of imitation, adaptation, and testing, which iterated repeatedly can move a company a long way from its original business model. Ultimately, this approach can gener-

ate a significant number of breakthrough products and business models.

4. A "good enough will do for now" attitude. This culture embodies the premise that products and processes can always be improved in the next cycle of change, and again, in the one after that.

5. Acceptance of "the Confucius inside." This is a culture of obedience within an accepted hierarchy in which top-down directives predominate, corporate outlooks are shaped by a single leader, and there is little or no debate at team level.

6. A "why not me?" view of success. This culture believes that individuals can succeed as entrepreneurs if given the opportunity, and that they can be as good, if not better, than those from anywhere else in the world.

At least for the moment, this culture serves Chinese companies well. And in part, it has worked because of the country's unprecedented economic growth; the Chinese have their own version of the saying "A rising tide lifts all boats." By moving rapidly, testing and experimenting, endlessly looking for new entrepreneurial opportunities, and producing goods that were just good enough to meet customers' needs and expectations, companies found they could thrive. Product quality was often poor, and most businesses lacked the time, knowledge, or resources to excel. Nevertheless, their "rough-and-tough" management style (known in Chinese as *cu fang xing guanli*) met the requirements of China's rapid market development and loose regulatory environment.

But this won't be sufficient to succeed in the future. It will eventually prove unsuitable for the global competitive landscape—and even for the Chinese business environment as it changes. Some Chinese business leaders are aware of this. They know that their companies can't continue along the same development path that has served them to date: markets are larger but far more open; consumers are wealthier but presented with an ever greater choice of goods and brands; and investment in infrastructure means that increasing numbers of competitors can reach into their markets.

Accordingly, these leaders recognize the need to improve their management capabilities and corporate governance, often radically rather than incrementally. Some are responding with redoubled efforts to produce whatever they make even more cheaply—by adding scale, by looking for ways to reduce costs still further, by searching for new markets both overseas and at home. Others are asking themselves whether a reliance on low costs alone is still viable, and if so, for how long. They want to do things differently, but wonder whether they can find the resources to develop the innovation skills needed to move up the value chain or find other ways to develop new, sustainable competitive advantages. Increasingly, they understand the importance of greater precision in management: specifically, the use of analysis and data to support decision making.

A case in point is Hengan, a very successful consumer company headquartered in Jinjiang in the southern part of Fujian Province. Established in 1985 and listed in Hong Kong in 1998, Hengan has become China's number-one player in the high-end tissue paper market and the number-two player in the sanitary napkin market. It is ahead of other multinational competitors such as APP, Kimberly-Clark, and Unicharm. Having a stated ambition of becoming an Rmb 10 billion ($1.5 billion) company in revenues, Hengan had already achieved Rmb 7 billion in 2008. By that time, its CEO, Xu Lianjie, had already led his company through two strategic transformations.

The first took place in 2001. While the company's senior management team was still basking in the glory of Hengan's Hong Kong listing and enjoying 10 percent annual growth, Xu became worried about the mismatch between his company's growing scale and the structure of its management system. Over the next eighteen months, he restructured most of Hengan's operating processes using total-cycle time techniques, which few, if any, other Chinese enterprises had adopted at that time. The outcome was a set of significant benefits in working practices that saw revenue growth jump from around 10 percent annually to 37 percent between 2003 and 2008, while profit growth averaged 36 percent.

In 2008, when most Hengan staff were once again anticipating another prosperous year, Xu turned his attention to strategic planning and supply-chain management. To maintain the company's growth rate he initiated a "second transformation," working with external consultants to develop new management systems for strategy and operations. Still in progress, this program includes a focus on installing systematic methods for identifying new growth opportunities.

As this story suggests, the leaders of China's most energetic companies, both state owned and private, are driven by lofty ambitions. They don't just want their companies to survive, or even just to grow and be profitable—they want them to achieve world-class status—and in the shortest possible time. They have seen this happen with companies such as Huawei, Haier, and to some extent, Lenovo, and many of them want to do the same. They may not fully understand all of the details and ramifications of what it means to be "world class," and what might be required to attain such status, but they will embrace any feasible change that will help them reach it.

A growing number of Chinese business leaders and entrepreneurs, like Xu Lianjie, recognize the shortcomings of their current business strategies and are all too aware that their current core competencies cannot help them sustain growth in the long run. They are more than willing to apply international best practices, even if that means having to change their own established ways of doing things. They are eager to learn about all the latest business and technology trends. Management books are enormously popular in China, usually displayed prominently in bookstores. Translations of Jack Welch's autobiography, Jim Collins's studies of successful companies, and other management classics are all long-standing bestsellers.

Chinese enterprise executives often talk about *yuguojijiegui*, adopting global business practices and establishing a stronger link to the outside world. At the same time, Chinese business leaders recognize that

China is and will remain somewhat distinctive. They are cautious about transplanting Western practices wholesale to the Chinese enterprise environment without any revision or adaptation.

If the challenge for Chinese companies is to become more global while retaining the strengths they developed at home, for multinationals the challenge is to become more Chinese while drawing on the advantages of their worldwide operations. The multinationals that have performed best in China have embraced the same qualities that have led domestic companies to success: entrepreneurship, experimentation, ambition, openness to alliances, attention to emerging markets, and—above all—an ability to move fast when they spot opportunities.

Successful multinationals will be entrepreneurial in drawing on the resources China offers: moving more elements of their value chains into China; looking for further advantages in its manufacturing industries, and the supply-chain networks that support them; exploring the potential for partnerships and R&D; and, of course, penetrating new markets as they emerge and grow across the country. In short, the most profitable companies may be those that mix the practices of entrepreneurial China with those of the world's best multinationals—a new China strategy.

CHAPTER 4

Official China

Visitors who don't read or speak Chinese may spend weeks, months, and even years in China without directly encountering the Communist Party. The experience of arriving at any of the country's major international airports—Beijing, say, or Pudong in Shanghai, or Guangzhou's Baiyun—is politically neutral. The posters calling for international proletarian unity were taken down long ago, and the symbols of communism largely discarded. The uniforms of immigration, police, and other security officials are hard to differentiate from those of many other countries.

Two decades of nonstop construction have created dynamic urban landscapes of steel, concrete, and glass—the sort of landscape that is typically associated with aggressive capitalism. China may have 5,000 years of history as a nation, but comparatively few places remain that evoke the past. Instead, downtown streets in large cities are lined with towering banks, hotels, and shopping plazas. Beijing has its magnificent stadium built to host the Olympics, Rem Koolhass's Central China Television headquarters, and the French-designed National Centre for the Performing Arts, more commonly known as the Egg. Not to be outdone, Shanghai has the Jin Mao Tower, designed by Chicago's Skidmore, Owings & Merrill, and its Grand Theatre, designed by France's Jean-Marie Charpentier.

Perhaps more astonishing than these architectural marvels is the view from the top of the taller buildings in any mid-sized Chinese city, such as Qingdao, Ningbo, Hohhot, Nanjing, Changsha, or Changchun. The vast majority of the buildings spread out below, certainly anything over five stories, have sprung up since Deng's southern tour in 1992. Even to those of us who have lived here and watched it take shape, China's newness is utterly startling.

The Chinese outlook on life mirrors its architecture. The politics that permeated everyday existence when Mao was alive have been put aside in the rush to create and enjoy prosperity. No longer are the Chinese people required to participate in one political campaign after another; no longer must they search out class enemies or counterrevolutionaries. Their interests and energies are concentrated on personal matters: work and study, travel and leisure, buying and maintaining a home, shopping for and enjoying the goods that pour forth from China's factories. Consumerism is as rampant here as in any capitalist country; the Chinese are increasingly being encouraged to spend more to help speed recovery from the global recession, and, to date, they haven't been remiss in their rush to purchase cars, computers, mobile phones, and flat-screen televisions.

Psychologically, this focus on and faith in the future has contributed to the intensity driving China—the urge to catch up with the world and once again become a leading center of global achievement. This is not to say that the country's past has been forgotten. The Chinese have enormous pride in the achievements of their country's inventors and explorers, artists and calligraphers, poets and novelists, and the grand sweep of its history. But the urge to move on is understandable. Many of the events of the past two centuries have been painful: China's nineteenth-century treatment at the hands of other countries and their armed forces, and then the internecine terrors of Mao's rule, particularly during the great step backward of the Cultural Revolution. China's progress, particularly since the early 1990s, can be attributed to the willingness of its people to put this history behind them, rightly or wrongly, rather than scrutinize the past to attribute blame or exact retribution.

Where's the Communist Party in all this? Its role in everyday life has declined enormously as the trend toward liberalization has extended far beyond the economy to the decisions of ordinary people. Throughout the past three decades, the party's desire to control every part of people's lives—from where they live to the career they choose to their lifestyles—has receded. It no longer assigns jobs and homes, restricts overseas travel to only a handful of people, or prevents the movement of people within the country. Of course, officialdom still exists, with all its myriad rules and regulations. But that is bureaucracy, which has a long and rich tradition in China, as opposed to outright control. Constraints remain, but these are mostly the economic limits of a developing nation; the political forces that from 1949 to the early 1980s took decision making out of the hands of most people have largely disappeared.

To many observers, especially Westerners, China's embrace of a market-based economy seems to have made the country capitalist in all but name and reduced the power of officials to control every aspect of people's lives. The country remains authoritarian, they argue, but surely where economic freedoms lead, political freedom will follow. After all, a population with a rapidly emerging middle class, exposed to external influences and ideas, and with an ever greater diversity of interests demanding some form of representation must inevitably move away from communism and toward democracy.

But they are wrong. China will remain a communist nation, at least for the foreseeable future. The Communist Party may be invisible to visitors and it may be less controlling that in the past, but its more than 70 million members continue to dominate every level of government and society, including universities, companies, the media, the army, police, and every civic body. If there's one thing its leaders are committed to, it is remaining the country's sole holders of political power. As unwaveringly as ever, they believe that China's development, both socially and economically, can only be achieved under the auspices of the Communist Party.

Thus, in addition to economic liberalization and the market and business environments, any China strategy must take into account the one other force determining the country's trajectory: official China. The role played by the government, and the Communist Party within the government, is immense. Officials continue to direct the country, both socially and economically, in ways that often seem opaque to foreigners. The starting point for a better understanding is the goals, motives, and methods of China's leaders.

Anatomy of a Political Agenda

Despite the massive economic and social changes, the top priorities of China's leaders have remained almost unchanged since Deng launched reform at the end of the 1970s. They are economic growth, social stability, and continued Communist Party rule.

For Deng and his successors, maintaining the rule of the Communist Party has been the sine qua non of their agenda. After the disastrous years of the Cultural Revolution, Deng realized that the key to ensuring party rule and rebuilding China's strength was to raise the national living standards. Doing so would both justify the party's right to rule and allow it to regain popular support.

Thus through the 1980s and 1990s, official China followed a single mantra: "What is good for growth is good for China." Farms were transformed into economic zones, city residents were uprooted to make way for highways, migrants from distant provinces were brought in to man assembly lines, foreign investment was welcomed, and banks were forced to make loans for machinery and equipment—all in pursuit of growing GDP.

Progress was not always smooth. The student-led democracy movement of 1989 revealed a widespread discontent with inflation and corruption. For Deng, however, although the protests represented a threat to social stability and the party's authority, they also demonstrated why getting the economy right was vital to the long-term survival of the Communist Party. So after overseeing the suppression of the protests and the brief period of economic stagnation that followed, Deng resumed his calls for radical economic reform, albeit with greater attention to ideological education and the prevention of the emergence of new threats to Communist Party rule.

The economic expansion that followed vindicated Deng's decision. But by the year 2000, it was becoming clear that many problems had been brushed aside in the country's rush for growth. Wages had soared in the cities, but they had stagnated in the countryside. Inland regions had been left behind while the coastal regions prospered. Health care, education, and other social welfare provisions had lagged badly. The environmental damage being inflicted on the country was reaching crisis proportions. And, in the general rush to become rich fast, corruption had flourished.

By 2002, when Hu Jintao became the chief of China's Communist Party, it was clearly time for a change of emphasis. Official China needed a new mindset, one that emphasized a far greater range of values than economic growth alone. It came with the unveiling that year of a new goal for China: the establishment of a "harmonious society" that would be achieved using the principles of a "scientific perspective."

To many people outside China, such phrases sound vague and meaningless. Their adoption, however, marked a major shift in outlook at the top of the Communist Party, one aimed at addressing the many dissatisfactions emerging in a society where some people prospered much more than others. Quickly, it became clear that the single-minded emphasis on growth that dominated the first stage of China's economic development would be replaced with a more holistic approach. Strengthening the economy, although still a vital task, would henceforth be balanced with other priorities; at the top of the list was reducing the various inequalities that had built up, especially those that threatened to lead to social unrest. The new outlook also embraced other areas, from more environmentally conscious industrial policies (discouraging the further development of resource-intensive industries; promoting energy efficiency; and fostering exploration of alternative and renewable energy sources) to increased spending on education and health care to new laws strengthening workers' rights.

In addition to a more sustainable development model, China's political leaders have been reworking their approach to governance. Their goal is to ensure greater public support for the Communist Party, and thus to give it legitimacy and reinforce the party's hold on power. The largest changes have been concentrated in two areas: improving effectiveness by strengthening the Communist Party's organization and raising the standards for admitting members; and enhancing the government's ability to direct and respond to public opinion. These two areas are worth examining in detail because they demonstrate official China's seriousness and thoroughness of purpose, and its commitment to maintaining both social stability and the current political system.

Through the 1990s and early 2000s, the Communist Party directed its research institutes to study the longevity of political parties. The collapse of socialist rule in the Soviet Union and Eastern Europe was examined as was the continued success of parties such as Japan's Liberal Democratic Party and Singapore's People's Action Party. In a fascinating examination of these studies, David Shambaugh, a professor who specializes in the internal workings of the Chinese Communist Party, lists the conclusions that official China took from them:[1]

- Don't let the economy stagnate; maintain growth and keep living standards rising.
- Keep the economy open to the rest of the world; continue absorbing the best techniques of capitalism, be they managerial practices or technologies.

- Strengthen the Communist Party's organization, particularly where its powers have been weakened, such as in the countryside, or where they never existed, such as within private and foreign-invested enterprises.
- Maintain strict control over the media; use it to promote desired views and restrict the spread of dissent.
- Be wary of Western attempts to undermine Communist Party rule; counter these wherever necessary.

These were all areas that the communist parties of the Soviet bloc had neglected. Not wanting to follow them into oblivion, the Chinese Communist Party has paid attention to all of them. It has established new local committees in organizations and communities ignored during the 1980s, and reinvigorated committees that had withered. In a monumental human resources initiative, the party assessed every one of its tens of millions of members. Older, poorly educated officials were retired, and younger ones promoted to replace them. Training courses were created. And the party broadened its membership base—including, since 2001, private businesspeople.

The party simultaneously undertook a massive effort to strengthen its ability to monitor and shape public opinion. Aware that the developments of the past three decades have created a society that is far more diverse, with wide-ranging interests, official China has studied the persuasive techniques of marketing and public relations, including the techniques of "spin" used in Western democracies. Opinion polls and surveys are regularly conducted. City governments set up websites to keep their citizens informed about their actions and established telephone hotlines for complaints and comments.

Most interesting of all is official China's new approach to oversight of the media, which represents almost a 180-degree turnaround from the brainwashing of traditional communism. Using the media it controls directly, particularly television, the government delivers messages that it wants to get across. These might emphasize China's achievements, particularly its economic ones. The government also restricts the dissemination of messages that it deems counterproductive. At the same time, however, an enormous degree of freedom has been granted to media companies that produce publications, broadcasts, and websites devoted to entertainment, lifestyle, sports, and other nonpolitical subjects.

This has resulted in an explosion in the volume and quality of Chinese media. Career opportunities that never existed before have opened to those who want to work in broadcasting or print. And those working in media know that most of the time, on most subjects, they can say whatever they want, provided they don't cross clearly delineated boundaries. Similar demarcations exist elsewhere for academics, artists, musicians, authors, and so on. Governmental oversight and control is maintained via regulations and laws, monitoring, and, most significantly, the self-interest of the players, who have no wish to lose their status and newfound freedom.

Official China's new approach to media might, and does, seem strange and discomfiting to people who grew up with a tradition of free speech and free press. But in the context of its predecessor, it has created notable change on at least three fronts. Socially, the country has a media and cultural life with a variety that is more responsive to people's needs, tastes, and interests than ever before. Commercially, the way has opened for an enormous expansion in the media industries. And, politically, the government and the Communist Party have enhanced their image as the protectors and promoters of the Chinese people and Chinese culture.

In short, official China has moved from being a "hard" manager to being a "softer" one. Just as economic management has shifted from a command-and-control model to one where market forces determine most decisions, official China's social management has come to rely on indirect techniques of persuasion rather than repression. In September 2009, *Newsweek* quoted Brookings scholar Cheng Li on this new aspect of the party; he said it was "a substantial change" related to the shift in party leadership from an older generation trained in engineering to a younger cohort trained in law, economics, and history.[2]

At heart, this represents another step in the continuing metamorphosis of the Communist Party's identity. It began as a revolutionary party with a mission to capture and hold power. Now it is a governing party, whose primary task is the management of society. No longer does it see itself, as it did under Mao, as a party that represents the interests of just one stratum of society—the peasantry and the working class. Instead, its task has become the governing of society as a whole.

Hu Jintao's declaration that China's goal should be the establishment of a harmonious society marked the official recognition of this transformation. Underlying this notion is an acknowledgment that as Chinese society has grown more complex, its government must continually earn its authority by improving the lives of the Chinese people and by reconciling conflicting interests and demands. The government has embraced the idea that prosperity brought about by economic reform can be shared equitably—but only if the state is involved in determining and shaping the nation's direction and development, which in turn requires better governance skills. From this perspective, the Communist Party remains as vital to China's future as ever. In addition, China's leaders believe that to maintain relevance and legitimacy, they must recover and expand China's standing in the world. This is why they now emphasize China rather than communism.

Although there are still those who predict the collapse of official China, all evidence points in the opposite direction. By most measures, China remains authoritarian, and there is no sign that this will change. For Western advocates of human rights, the restrictions that continue to exist in China will thus remain unacceptable. But the fact is that the Chinese people have far more freedom in almost every area of life than ever before. Many people, probably the vast majority of the population, don't just passively accept their country's political system, but actively support it, in a way that goes far beyond anything that propaganda or repression could induce. This is confirmed by surveys, such as a 2008 survey by the Pew Research Center, which concludes that the satisfaction levels of the Chinese people with their government and their lives ranks among the world's highest.[3]

Three Decisions That Shaped China

This kind of change, made in just a few years, is not just a remarkable political shift, but also a noteworthy recalibration of one of the world's largest governments. Official China accomplished it through three critical decisions; decisions that still influence the way it operates and that will continue to shape the way it meets the challenges of the next few years:

- *Step-by-step incremental change.* Over the past two decades, China's leaders have faced one set of problems after another and made progress—enormous progress in many instances—toward resolving or ameliorating almost all of them. They have overseen the dismantling of a centrally planned economy and its replacement with a largely market-driven one. They have maintained relative social stability, despite the internal migration of more than 100 million people around the country and the continuing political tensions in Tibet and Xinjiang. The country's financial system is far more robust than it was two decades ago, despite often-voiced fears that it faced an imminent meltdown. And the Communist Party has made itself into an institution whose legitimacy, and thus its potential for longevity, looks stronger than ever before.

  Government leaders take enormous pride in these achievements, and they conclude, with some justification, that one reason for their continued success is that they remain wedded to a gradual and incremental approach, even to changes that shake China's economic, social, and political fabric. Official China moves, as Deng once put it, by "crossing the river by feeling the stones." Throughout the reform era, China's leaders have avoided any kind of "big bang" approach for tackling problems. Instead, they have preferred to carefully prepare for change, use a range of administrative measures to test the way forward, and then execute change in stages over several years.

The restructuring of China's SOEs, described in chapter 3, exemplifies this incremental approach. Although led by Zhu Rongji, this reordering of the Chinese economy wasn't executed with a simple top-down order from the central government to local authorities; it was accomplished in stages. The first stage lasted through the entire 1980s, as the government eased the transition from state-set prices to market-based prices, abolished central planning's allocation of inputs and setting of outputs, and allowed incentives aimed at encouraging a managerial focus on profitability. In the early 1990s, fiscal reforms ended the reliance on state enterprises as the sole source of government revenues, severing the ties between companies and officials. And with the passing of China's Company Law in 1994, the SOEs were permitted to shift to private ownership.

As a result of this incremental approach, companies had both the mechanisms and incentives to go their own way, and governments, particularly local ones, had the mechanisms and incentives to let them do this or, in the case of loss-making businesses, shut them down. The result (though the word wasn't used) was privatization—sometimes through the sale of enterprises, more often by transferring ownership to their managers or officials.

There were losers in this process, especially in the industrial cities of north and northeast China, where millions of workers were sent home as their companies were closed, sold, or slimmed down. But there were also many beneficiaries: people with an entrepreneurial bent who found themselves owning or running companies, employees who worked for them, and—most important of all—

Chinese consumers, who, because these newly entrepreneurial companies existed, found the available range of goods broader and their quality better than ever before.

Another seemingly intractable problem that official China solved through step-by-step incremental change was the phenomenal burden that nonperforming loans placed on the nation's banking system. By the late 1990s, bad debt at China's banks had grown to account for 40 percent of all outstanding loans.

The Asian financial crisis of the late 1990s, and the problems it revealed in economies across the region, led officials to act. First, in 1998, the government recapitalized the country's four largest banks. The following year, it created four asset management companies that bought nonperforming loans from the big four banks at full face value. This was followed, from 2000 to 2005, with repeated rounds of restructuring, additional sales and write-downs of bad loans, and another series of recapitalizations funded by the country's foreign exchange reserves. The total cost to the government: $300 billion.[4]

Throughout the process, skeptical observers, especially foreigners, declared that these measures were not radical enough, pointing out that they involved nothing more than shuffling bad debts from one place to another. The critics missed the relentless pressure that official China put on banks to improve management practices, lessen the influence of local officials over lending decisions, lay off unnecessary staff, and close unneeded branches.

Stripped of their biggest headache, streamlined, and lending into a fast-growing economy, China's big banks found themselves transformed. Within seven years, they went from being technically insolvent to hugely profitable. In 2005 and 2006, three of the country's four largest banks—China Construction Bank, Bank of China, and Industrial and Commercial Bank of China—were successfully listed on international stock markets. (The fourth large state-owned bank, Agricultural Bank of China, continues to be problematic compared to the others, and it is the only one not to have been granted a stock market listing.) The $19 billion raised by Industrial and Commercial Bank of China via its simultaneous listing in Hong Kong and Shanghai in 2006 remains the world's largest initial public offering to date.

As for the bad loans, burying them in government-controlled asset management companies meant they couldn't blow up the financial system, as has happened with subprime mortgages in the United States. And although this bad debt still exists, its proportion relative to the overall economy has declined rapidly in the face of China's high growth rate.

• *Saying no to laissez-faire.* The rapid expansion in the role of market forces in the 1990s, particularly during Zhu Rongji's tenure as premier, led many to believe that official China's goal was essentially capitalist. It was not—and it is not. As described in chapter 3, the government has retained control over China's largest, most strategic industries and companies. Under Hu Jintao's leadership, this commitment has hardened. Thus, although market forces are still regarded as crucial to the efficient operation of the Chinese economy, official China's ultimate goal is clearly not a laissez-faire economy. Markets are a useful tool for economic development, not an end in themselves. Thus, while the country's economic reforms will continue, the pace of reform will almost certainly slow down in the late 2000s and early 2010s.

To understand why the government takes this tack, it is necessary to balance China's recent successes against the challenges that still confront it. Official China sees extraordinarily complex management problems wherever it looks. Making the economy sustainable requires tackling a whole series of issues, including pollution, the depletion of land, water, and other natural resources, and the overreliance on coal as an energy source. (The use of coal exacerbates the threat of climate change, especially at China's scale, while abandoning coal would raise concerns about energy security.) If urbanization isn't to result in the creation of shantytowns or an urban underclass, local governments must address employment, education, and health care. There is also the looming problem of an aging population, brought on in large part by the success of the one-child family policy that was introduced in 1979 (and is still in place in most of China today). Ethics are yet another area of concern: as China's society goes through massive upheaval, traditional values have lost their strength, as manifested most obviously in widespread corruption.

As China's political leaders consider these issues, the only conclusion they will come to is that the state will have to be more involved in the management of society, including the economy. Industries that the state deems strategic will continue to remain largely off-limits to foreign companies—and to non-state-owned Chinese companies as well.

Indeed, the key to official China will be the Chinese government's guiding of industry development and enterprise behavior. Already, there have been signs of a more hands-on industrial policy in industries, such as automobiles. The explicit goal is to turn China into a viable global competitor in these areas. In 2009, China spent $733 million of its economic stimulus on subsidizing and promoting the sale of small cars and trucks in rural areas, and another $220 million to fund R&D on green automotive technology. It is explicitly promoting mergers and consolidation among China's many automotive companies and trying to develop a platform of regulatory policies from which companies like BYD can more easily launch global initiatives.[5]

Even as it encourages companies to grow, official China has made it clear that it will prevent the emergence of tycoons or oligarchs of the kind that dominate the Russian economy. While economic reforms have allowed some businesspeople to become very wealthy, by retaining the key parts of the economy in state hands, the government has prevented the formation of a possible power base for a challenge to Communist Party rule.

Another indicator of increased government oversight is the drive, since 2008, to improve the legal environment and make business-related policies more transparent and universal. The multiple government authorities that once oversaw business regulation have been streamlined and made more efficient. This demonstrates Official China's continued commitment to a robust economy and business-friendly governance, even as it solidifies its position.

- *Greater global engagement.* China's economic needs—for resources, markets, technology, and expertise—mean that it has no alternative to becoming more globally engaged. Foreign investment will continue to be welcomed, with the opening of the economy, both internally and internationally, remaining a core part of government policy.

In the past, the globalization of China's economy was an inbound process, with companies from around the world coming to the country. In the next decade and beyond, it will also be an outbound process, with China's companies (and, increasingly, their technological, management, and financial capital and expertise) going out into the world. This is an issue that Hu Jintao has had to confront in a way his predecessors didn't. China's international ties grew through the 1980s and 1990s, but both Deng Xiaoping and Jiang Zemin, the country's Communist Party chief from 1989 until 2002 (and its president from 1993 to 2003), made a point of keeping a low global profile.

Since Hu became the country's top leader, however, China's growing economy and ever-increasing trade volume has meant having to engage with the world in a more demonstrative and influential way. China has had to find new sources of energy and raw materials in Australia, Africa, and South America; to maintain the stability of trade routes in the Pacific and Indian oceans; and to manage the increasingly complex economic and political rivalry and alliance it maintains with the United States, Japan, and Europe.

Hu's response has been to match his call for a harmonious society at home with a call for programs of peaceful development internationally, and an insistence that China's growing economic and political power should be perceived by other countries, especially in Asia, as an opportunity for mutual advancement, not a threat to their well-being. It's a call that will be heard repeatedly through the next decade and beyond as China's leaders spend far more time overseas, attending global summits, wooing state leaders, and smoothing the way for the global expansion of domestic companies.

In almost every area of international significance, it will not be possible for other countries to ignore China. Correspondingly, China will find it impossible to make major decisions, including domestic decisions, without considering their global ramifications. Isolation from the world is no longer an alternative for official China.

Engaging with Official China

For companies doing business in China, the implications of official China's strategy are mixed, but the situation is broadly positive. It is crucial for corporate leaders to figure out how the government's outlook will translate into policy and attitudes within individual industries and sectors, particularly those where the government is pursuing reform but also maintaining strong oversight.

China's banking sector, which is clearly a strategic industry, exemplifies many of the issues that the government faces, and the direction it is likely to take. Since China was admitted to the World Trade Organization in 2001, there has been an ongoing process of restricted liberalization. Under the oversight of the China Banking Regulatory

Commission, the sector's main architect, China has developed an increasingly strong and sophisticated banking system. Competition has been permitted, but subject to strict control, especially when foreign banks had a major advantage. This partial liberalization has allowed foreign banks to introduce modern banking practices, particularly at domestic banks in which they have purchased stakes. And there has been some integration with the global financial system.

China's banking system is built around the four big state-owned banks (Agricultural Bank of China, Bank of China, China Construction Bank, and Industrial and Commercial Bank of China) and supported by a series of smaller national and regional banks. The commission has allowed competition where it believes this will strengthen performance, but also maintained protection where necessary. Although it has eased some measures, such as the requirement that a nearly $50 million deposit be paid before a branch is opened, it has also held the expansion plans of foreign banks subject to its approval. Thus, although China's banking sector has been liberalized in theory, it remains one with high barriers to entry and multiple obstacles to growth.

Since late 2006, foreign banks can offer the same range of services and products as Chinese banks. Ownership restrictions have also eased: a foreign institution can now own up to 20 percent of any Chinese bank, as long as the total stake held by foreign institutions in a Chinese bank does not exceed 25 percent. Foreign banks can operate under their own names, but to build out a national branch network, they must incorporate in China and then negotiate a tough and expensive approvals system that leaves most of the control over particular products and practices with the government's officials. For various products, foreign banks are not allowed to operate on their own: credit cards, for example, can only be offered via a joint venture with a Chinese bank. And it would be very unlikely to see a foreign bank permitted to introduce an investment innovation before its Chinese counterparts.

Many international banks have established a presence in China, but only two have attempted to establish branch networks of any scale. The

UK's HSBC (which was founded in the 1860s in Hong Kong) has branches in twenty cities, and it has also taken a stake in Bank of Communications, China's fifth-largest bank, and Bank of Shanghai, one of the country's largest regional banks.[6] Citigroup has branches in eight cities, plus stakes in two city-level commercial banks: Shanghai Pudong Development Bank and Guangdong Development Bank.

Despite their clear commitment to China, the progress of both banks was slow, even before the global financial crisis. Official approval for Citigroup's purchase of a stake in Guangdong Development Bank took more than a year, and plans to increase its network to thirty branches by 2008 never came close to being realized. As for HSBC, its hopes of being allowed to expand its stake in Bank of Communications beyond the 20 percent limit have receded since it paid $1.75 billion to buy into the bank in 2004.

Other foreign banks have tried to establish a presence by buying stakes in Chinese banks. The largest deals involved the four largest Chinese banks with international stock market listings. These include the $3 billion spent by Bank of America for 9 percent of China Construction Bank in 2005, the $2.6 billion paid by Goldman Sachs for 5.75 percent of Industrial and Commercial Bank of China in 2006, and the $1.5 billion paid by Royal Bank of Scotland (RBS) for 4.3 percent of Bank of China in 2004. In addition, a host of banks from around the world have taken stakes in second-tier and regional banks, usually paying several tens or hundreds of millions of dollars.

But after the global financial crisis of 2008 and 2009, most of the givens that appeared to be shaping China's banking liberalization appeared to be rethought. Chinese officials have tightened regulatory procedures and clearly no longer see the Western financial system as an attractive model for their own system. Various stakes taken by foreign banks have been sold back, often by Western banks that needed to bolster their balance sheets. In January 2009, RBS sold its stake in Bank of China for $2.4 billion; a nice profit, but little more than a drop in the ocean of RBS's losses. The same month, Bank of America sold part of its Chinese holdings for $2.8 billion. It is likely that other troubled foreign banks will follow suit as the lock-in periods on their stakes in Chinese banks expire.

Aside from the financial straits in which many foreign banks find themselves, there are other reasons why inbound investment in China's banks may slow down. The dearth of stock market listings since 2008 means that there is less money to be made from IPO (initial public offering) fees. For retail banks, the prospects of establishing a branch network of any scale look as daunting as ever. And there is no indication—rather the opposite, in fact—that officials will consider easing the limits on foreign stakes in Chinese banks.

Finally, China's maintenance of a nonconvertible currency remains the largest single barrier to the integration of Chinese banks into the global financial system. Economists may argue the macroeconomic benefits of an international currency, but after witnessing the events of Asia's financial crisis and now the global financial meltdown, official China is wary of the problems that might occur if the government was to loosen its control over the renminbi (Rmb).

The internationalization of China's banking system, therefore, is far more likely to come from outbound investments made by Chinese banks in foreign banks. So far, there have been only a handful of small foreign purchases, the exception being the £1.5 billion stake that China Development Bank (one of the country's "policy" banks and, so, more a government arm than a bank in any normal usage of the word) bought in Britain's Barclays Bank in 2007. Another example would be the 20 percent stake in Standard Bank, Africa's largest bank bought by the Industrial and Commercial Bank of China (ICBC) in 2007 for $5.6 billion.

Going forward, however, Chinese banks, especially the larger ones, are likely to expand outbound investment in foreign financial institutions. This will happen gradually at first, and with due attention to the shortcomings exposed in the world financial system since the start of the sub-prime mortgage crisis, but their investments will grow in size as they become more confident in their abilities to manage their purchases.

When all of these small, gradual, and incremental changes are considered together, it's clear that China's banking system has been transformed beyond recognition. In the next decade, there will be further progress with increasing competition, liberalized ownership and product rules, and global integration. But this will only occur with strict official oversight. Indeed, it is quite likely that China's financial system will become *both* more liberal and more subject to central control—with greater competition allowed among banks and more government direction over their lending and credit policies.

Other industries will follow a similar path: liberalization for the benefits it brings, subjected to oversight and, ultimately, control by the government and Communist Party. Official China has a series of goals in almost every industry. If foreign companies seem ready to help realize these goals, then they will be allowed to participate, especially if they can bring expertise and technology that will help raise standards in the short to medium term and allow Chinese companies to establish themselves in the longer term. China's leaders are prepared to offer immediate, albeit controlled, access to the country's markets, partly for the short-term benefits—jobs, faster growth, and a wider range of goods—that contribute to social stability and satisfaction with the government, and even more so for the longer-term strategic gains they bring to China's aspiration of becoming a powerful country with a modern economy. Companies that do not understand this reality—and that fail to recognize the importance of officials' belief that ultimately everything in China must come under their direction—run the risk of seeing potential but never realizing it.

Recent developments in worker's rights and tax reform highlight official China's strategic direction. The Labor Contract Law, brought into force in 2008, significantly strengthened the rights of staff and workers. It stipulates that all employees are entitled to a written employment contract and makes it much harder to lay off and fire them. Although many companies have complained that the new law will add significantly to their costs, in official China's view, it is fully in line with the ideal of a "harmonious society." In the rush to expand manufacturing capacity, workers had often seen their interests come second to those of factory owners; redressing this imbalance was clearly important, especially for a government that claims a particular affinity with working people.

More than this, the new legislation enables official China to extend its power by rule of law as opposed to direct governmental edict. Previously, the government commanded that something be done and enforced compliance with sanctions. In developing a legal infrastructure, the state can devolve its powers, retaining oversight, but allowing those involved to police themselves. Written employment contracts, for example, allow employees to monitor their rights themselves. Providing that they can depend on the state for enforcement, such a system will enhance both official China's legitimacy and its control.

China's political leaders are also using tax reform to strengthen their governance abilities. China began building a Western-style tax system to meet the needs of its market economy in the mid-1990s. While development has been rapid, unsurprisingly, many loopholes remain. As a result, for much of the past two decades, many companies, both Chinese and foreign, have had a relatively free ride in terms of taxes.

This is ending as the government improves and modernizes its revenue raising abilities. Transfer pricing provides a notable example of the changes under way. Until recently, tax officials had a very limited ability to track how companies priced goods they moved from one subsidiary to another. This enabled many firms to spirit exports out of China tax free and save themselves billions of dollars in the process. (This explains, in part, why foreign-invested enterprises, especially those from Hong Kong and Taiwan, have long reported lower profit levels than other companies in China.)

Since the mid-2000s, however, the State Administration of Taxation has devoted increasing attention to this issue. It is training inspectors to conduct transfer-pricing audits, and promulgating several sets of regulations and procedures. So far, its capacity to audit companies remains minute; fewer than one hundred companies are scrutinized each year. But official China plans to bring nearly three decades of loose tax regulation and enforcement to an end. Within a few years, and quite likely far sooner than most companies expect, China will have a well-developed capacity for handling transfer pricing as well as other taxation issues. Companies should prepare themselves for compliance.

As with workers' rights, this control is being imposed without the arbitrary intervention of officials in the direct operations of companies. And in both instances, the net outcome is the tightening of the Communist Party's hold on China's economy.

The Future of Official China

It is a mistake to think of China as being in a transitional stage politically. The China the world sees now is the one that will exist for at least the next decade, and quite likely well beyond that. In almost every area of governance, reforms are under way, aimed at improving official China's performance, making it more responsive and flexible, more effective and resilient, and better equipped both to protect and project the national interests. Some reforms will lead to an increase of freedom, but others will lead to tighter oversight. The overall goal will remain the preservation of official China's current system, not its replacement.

This creates something of a challenge for the nations of the West. Ever since the collapse of the Soviet Union, Westerners, and Americans in particular, have assumed that multiparty democracies and laissez-faire markets will eventually triumph worldwide. The global financial crisis may have shaken this conviction, but it hasn't fundamentally altered it. China's development trajectory, however, suggests there is an alternative: countries can build a powerful economy by allowing market forces a sizable, but ultimately limited, role, and populations can support the government and economy without being granted political representation.

Whether this is a model for others to emulate is debatable. It is deeply rooted in China's specific economic and social conditions, so it may not be easily transferable. But official China believes that there is no reason to change political systems, and most of the Chinese people agree with them. In their eyes, the system works; it may not be perfect, but particularly since the early 1990s, it has delivered. The living standards for the vast majority of the population have risen (in some cases, enormously), and personal freedoms and opportunities have grown to an extent unimaginable a generation ago. While many Chinese criticize the Communist Party in their daily conversations, in the same way that Americans casually criticize American political parties, they believe that their country is reemerging as a global power in large part because of the guidance that the Communist Party exercises over society; and that the party's influence throughout Chinese society is a desirable factor, if not a prerequisite of China's continued development.

This does not mean that the Communist Party will be fully immune to external change in the future. The rise of personal freedom and enabling technologies, such as the Internet, will result in the increased scrutiny of leaders and their actions at all levels. And with the world becoming ever more interconnected, not just economically, but also politically, other external pressures will appear that are difficult to fully foresee today.

And in some ways, China's strong central control may prove to be a boon for the West. For instance, with regard to climate change, official China's ability to unilaterally impose strict environmental controls may give it an advantage over Western nations, which need to secure the consent of electorates.

For business leaders, negotiating relationships with official China will require a depth and subtlety of understanding that goes far beyond the sloganeering that characterizes much discussion of China's politics. It is a mistake to let the authoritarian side of China's political system block engagement with the Chinese government. Instead, businesses should keep an eye on the two balancing acts that Chinese leaders must maintain. Domestically, they have to respond to people's needs and desires while attempting to shape them; internationally, they must be engaged with other countries while protecting their own sovereignty. Although the Communist Party may remain invisible to most visitors, it continues to be omnipresent. As it moves toward a rule whose resilience is based more on responsiveness than repression, it may well create a new form of government entirely: an omnipresent, benign, market-supporting, outward-looking, business-enabling authoritarian regime.

CHAPTER 5

One World

Iℕ 2006, IBM ᴜᴘʀᴏᴏᴛᴇᴅ its global procurement headquarters, transferring them from Somers in New York State, twenty miles north of its headquarters at Armonk, to Shenzhen in south China's Pearl River Delta, just across the border from Hong Kong. It was a notable moment: the first time one of IBM's core arms had left the United States. And it marked a significant move along the road toward making IBM a "globally integrated enterprise" running "truly global systems of production," as its CEO, Sam Palmisano, had written in *Foreign Affairs* the same year.[1]

IBM had first arrived in south China just over a decade earlier, opening an office there in 1993. In 1994, the company set up its first joint venture in Shenzhen, making personal computers. During the next decade, this operation was followed by others—producing ThinkPad laptops, servers, retail store systems, storage devices, and printers. By the early 2000s, the city was home to 2,000 employees, with another 6,000 working for IBM elsewhere in China.[2]

As IBM's Chinese presence grew, thousands of other companies became its suppliers, and suppliers to other computer manufacturers as well. They joined a variety of sourcing networks stretching across Shenzhen and the other cities of the Pearl River Delta. Many of these companies supplied parts and materials for low-end light industrial goods: toys, sports shoes, plastic products, and so on. Others provided components for higher-end information technology, computing and telecommunications equipment. To support the region's electronics assembly industry came other component makers from elsewhere in Asia, and with them came the emerging giants of global electronics outsourcing, firms such as Taiwan's Foxconn-Hon Hai, Singapore's Flextronics, and Solectron from the United States.

Other businesses, especially from Hong Kong, rolled out the logistics and supporting technology needed to coordinate the transport of parts and materials and the dispatch of finished goods. As they did, local officials oversaw the expansion of economic zones and industrial parks, the building of highways and container ports, the opening of new universities and training colleges, and the arrival of migrant labor from other parts of the country.

By the time IBM exited the personal computers business—selling its PC arm, including its ThinkPad laptop business, to Lenovo in 2005—the Pearl River Delta region had remade itself into the heart of the world's most important technology supply chain. Clustered there were nearly all the companies that produced the world's electronic and IT goods. Wherever the individual components of any product were made—in Taiwan, Japan, Malaysia, Singapore, or, as was increasingly the case, in China itself—they would be brought together and assembled in a factory somewhere in the Delta.

IBM's executives thoroughly understood the structure and capabilities of the networks that comprised this supply chain. They also knew that the region had become home to one of the largest pools of procurement talent worldwide. Moving its own procurement arm there not only strengthened its own supply base, but also positioned the company to help clients strengthen their own supply chains, one of the core focuses of IBM's business.

At the same time, 1,200 miles north in Beijing, IBM was developing another group of China-based talent. In 1995, the company founded its China Research Laboratory, one of just eight such centers worldwide set up to tap into local reservoirs of high-tech expertise. It is based in the city's Zhongguancun Software Park, next to Beijing's main university district; most of its more than 150 researchers hold doctorates or masters degrees from Beijing, Tsinghua, or other leading Chinese universities. Today, IBM's lab specializes in speech and language technologies, cross-border e-business solutions, and pervasive computing: the embedding of microprocessors in every-day objects. Every year, some 1,800 researchers apply to join it; only a few are selected. Until recently, IBM hired three researchers in the United States and one each in Switzerland, Japan, Israel, and India each year. Then in 2008, the company opened a new research facility in Shanghai, its first in a decade. Starting with just over a dozen researchers, it is due to have a hundred in place, working principally on Internet-related topics such as cloud computing and Web-delivered services. Today, IBM runs all of its global growth business out of Shanghai. This includes its business in Asia, Latin America, Russia, Eastern Europe, the Middle East, and Africa.

IBM still produces hardware in China. And it also has a thriving Chinese business in services; in 2009, despite the global economic slowdown, IBM's consulting arm forecast a doubling in size of its China operations within a year because of growing demand from Chinese companies. To meet this demand, IBM plans to open four new China offices, taking its total presence from six to ten.[3] But although China's low prices are still attractive to IBM, that's not why the company has placed its labs in Beijing and Shanghai or its procurement HQ in Shenzhen. They are there because, for IBM, those are the best places for them to be, both to support its clients and to offer services to other of the company's divisions and operations around the world. China is the site for several different nodes of Sam Palmisano's globally integrated enterprise.

Two-Way Globalization

Removing the boundaries that inhibit integration is, in a sense, the definition of globalization. Thanks to the advances of information, communications, transport, and other technologies, combined with the lowering of political barriers to international trade and investment, the world has become a far smaller, more interconnected place. This perspective is, no doubt, familiar to readers of this book; it was popularized by *New York Times* columnist and author Thomas L. Friedman in his 2005 book *The World Is Flat* and by the Japanese strategy writer and thinker Kenichi Ohmae fifteen years earlier, in his book *The Borderless World.*[4] According to this view, companies in a globalized world can situate different parts of their business wherever they can find the right skills and abilities. The location of a company's headquarters need have little say about the distribution of its operations in countries worldwide. Instead, thanks to instant communications, anything that can be moved electronically—including capital, in-depth knowledge, human contact, data, and instructions—can be placed at any spot on the globe connected via fiber-optic cable, copper wire, or satellite to the Internet or other forms of electronic communication.

That multinationals with operations spanning the world have bought into this vision is no surprise; by their very nature, they are always looking for new sources of cross-border value. But the Chinese government and business leaders, and most of its citizens, have also bought into the same vision.

This represents a more dramatic shift than many people realize. In chapter 4, I noted that China's original intention when it first opened its doors to foreign investment was to control the world's influence, corralling it in special economic zones. Even today, it remains very much a developing nation; its per capita GDP, despite the growth of the last three decades, is still just one-fifteenth that of the United States, on a par with El Salvador and Namibia.

But it has also become the world's most connected nation, with more people using the Internet than any other country (more than 300 million,[5] compared with 220 million in the United States; India's 60 million pales in comparison), and more of them using broadband (120 million, or about half again as many as in the United States). Throw in its 1 billion phone users—550 million of them mobile subscribers—and it is clear that China's rulers have accepted the fact that the country's population can surf the World Wide Web, talk to each other openly, and exchange emails and text messages. The Chinese government still blocks or censors what it views as politically unacceptable websites. But, by and large, the Chinese people enjoy a level of freedom to communicate with each other that was not possible a decade ago. If we include the market-opening measures of China's World Trade Organization accession terms and other measures China has taken to free up trade and welcome investment, then there is certainly a strong case that China has not only embraced globalization vigorously, but made a remarkable transition from isolation to global engagement.

In the aftermath of the 2008 financial crisis, that openness is taking on new dimensions. As *Financial Times* columnist Martin Wolf noted in September 2009, "The west's reputation for financial and economic competence is in tatters, while that of China has soared."[6] Others have observed Chinese officials beginning to deliver advice and warnings to outside companies and governments, and to be treated with deference. For example, a group of Chinese diplomats admonished Peter Orszag, the director of the United States Office of Management and Budget, on the importance of health care reform, in part on the grounds that this would safeguard the value of U.S. government bonds in which the Chinese famously hold a $2 trillion investment, but also with a status directly related to weathering the crisis more successfully than other nations.[7]

To outsiders looking in, the benefits of globalization for China are abundantly clear. The benefits of Chinese globalization for multinational companies are also clear, not just for those using the country as a manufacturing or sourcing location, but for those like IBM, which have integrated their China operations into their global value chain.

There could even be great opportunities for companies entering China for the first time. With the emerging consumer culture in Tier 3 and 4 cities, there will be new potential in untapped markets, such as the service sectors. A company entering China could pick out one market category or consumer segment and have hundreds of thousands of potential customers. That could make China the largest market niche play opportunity in the history of the world.

From within, the view of what has happened might look rather different—so different it's worth briefly considering just how daunting and unfamiliar the changes of the last two decades might seem to an executive of a Chinese company who went to sleep in 1989 and woke up in 2009.

Since the government opened the country's doors to foreign business, barriers to competition have fallen relentlessly, and a nonstop stream of multinationals has flooded in. Many of them now dominate their sectors. Microsoft looks as much a behemoth in China as it does in Europe and America. KFC is ubiquitous on the streets of Chinese cities, far ahead of any Chinese fast-food chain. Procter & Gamble is the leading fast-moving consumer goods company. Tetra Pak, the Swedish company, is the leader in liquid packaging. Global accountancy companies, law firms, and consultancies, all with non-Chinese names, occupy the high ground of professional services. Coca-Cola and Pepsi dominate China's carbonated drinks sector.

Both state-owned and private companies find themselves under ever more intense pressure to be profitable, to find new markets, to add new skills, and to acquire new technologies. When they innovate, they find multinationals following in their paths, assimilating their techniques and methods. Huawei may have changed the global telecommunications equipment manufacturing business forever, but all the world's major equipment vendors now have operations in China, taking advantage of its low-cost production and research environment. Huawei's staff are now the targets for poaching, and its intellectual property is vulnerable to being stolen.

In short, one might expect Chinese business leaders to regard the outside world with concern, trepidation, and resentment, not unlike the way that incumbent company leaders in many countries feel about competitors from outside.

But most Chinese business leaders don't feel this way. They regard the outside world with curiosity and entrepreneurial zeal, even when it encroaches on their own markets. In short, they see the promise that the world holds for them. Foreign observers have paid a great deal of attention to the impact globalization has had on China. But the Chinese themselves are keenly aware of the potential they have to affect globalization itself. China's development over the next decade and beyond will shape the economic and perhaps the political landscape of the rest of the world.

Globalization, of course, is a two-way phenomenon. The combination of the scale and openness of China's markets, and its entrepreneurial drive (particularly in manufacturing and manufacturing-related services) will combine to propel Chinese products and ideas everywhere. And the channels through which globalization has flowed into China—investment and trade, and the interconnection of transportation and communications networks—will also carry China's influence back out to the global economy.

The rest of this chapter is about this impact, and how China's participation in the globalized economy will affect value chains, company structures, and corporate thinking on every continent.

The China-Enabled Global Company

Leaders of multinational companies may understand the need to do business in China, but few of them grasp the impact China will have on their operations in the rest of the world as China becomes integrated into the world economy. China is still typically viewed as a place "out there," a stand-alone location isolated from other aspects of global business.

That will change. While it is impossible to forecast exactly what changes will occur, it is possible to discern some key trends that will affect the restructuring of global companies.

One trend is the impact of innovation. As Chinese R&D becomes an ever richer source of new practices and knowledge, companies from around the world will draw upon the talent and innovations being realized in China. They will monitor the growing number of Chinese corporate research labs, particularly developments in their manufacturing and manufacturing-related skills.

The Chinese government's funding of research in key technology areas such as aerospace and information technology will also be a factor. China has already received more than two hundred orders for a 70- to 110-seat regional aircraft, the ARJ-21, being developed by a subsidiary of the state-owned Aviation Industry Corporation of China (AVIC). And in September 2009, AVIC unveiled its C919 commercial aircraft: the single-aisle plane is scheduled to make its first flight in 2014, be in commercial use by 2016, and compete directly with planes under development by Boeing and Airbus.[8] Inevitably, some of those innovations will migrate into competitor's designs.

Indeed, that migration is a perennial aspect of technological advance: it tends to break down borders. During the past twenty years, technological innovation has leaked from multinational companies to Chinese producers. Now, it is beginning to flow in the other direction. For example, Motorola, Alcatel-Lucent, Intel, and other leading IT and telecommunications equipment companies all have research and development operations in China, employing the same pool of technology graduates who constitute the core research staff at Huawei and other Chinese telecom equipment makers.

Another trend is the scale and speed of value-chain growth as it spreads from China to the rest of the world. The networks of manufacturers and suppliers within China have grown; they include not just Chinese companies, but companies from elsewhere operating in China and foreign companies funded by Chinese investment.

This expansion of value chains from China to the rest of the world will be further reinforced by the growth of China's own markets. As more companies produce goods and services for the Chinese domestic market, they will integrate their China operations with their global value chains. This combination of a market and value chain in a single country is unique; mastery of both will give companies advantages that can be taken worldwide. No other country is like China in this combination, and nowhere has it ever before been necessary to be involved like this.

As this trend develops, competition among value chains rather than just among companies will become increasingly important. For a company such as Dell or Lenovo, at the "dragon head" of a value chain, overseeing the migration and management of their suppliers and key customers will become of even more importance than it is now. And companies within a value chain will have an even greater incentive to ensure they maintain their position and the overall success of the lead company and its brands.

These value chains will increasingly be multinational themselves, bringing together companies from China and other countries in unprecedented networks of businesses that cross national lines. Whether such an intermingling would lead to less national rivalry is hard to foresee, but it is hard to envisage this level of global integration existing without an impact on international relations. Politically, China and the United States may be rivals, but the relationship between the two (and between China and Europe) will be very different from the Cold War confrontation between the West and the Soviet Union. That was a zero-sum game—if one side won, the other lost—with no integration between the two sides. China's relationship with the West and other countries will be very different because of their unprecedented integration in the global economy.

These two trends—the increase in R&D and the further development of global value chains—favor what might be called "one world companies": international enterprises that can combine the best elements of international and Chinese operations in unified value chains, with each element—from research and development, through manufacturing and its attendant functions of sourcing and procurement, to distribution and marketing—in the most appropriate place for wherever they can find or create a market.

A growing number of these one world companies will be Chinese in origin. Moreover, China will play a disproportionate role in the development of one world companies, regardless of their country of origin. They will all have in common an ability to take advantage of the growth in scale of China's markets, of its growing dominance of various parts of the value chain for many goods, of its pools of expertise and talent, and of its integration into global communications and transport networks.

Companies with one world status will take advantage of the strengths of each major region. The United States will remain a giant consumer market, the financial crisis notwithstanding, and the source of other functions such as R&D and management innovation. Europe will also be a powerful market, although it is less dynamic than America. Japanese manufacturers will be a formidable force for decades to come, but Japan's preoccupations will be internal rather than international in the coming decades, as it tackles the issue of managing a graying population. India will be a significant market and source of business, particularly in software and services, but it will not come close to China as a market or production base for some years. It has yet to show a potential for evolving the sort of manufacturing sector that China developed in the 1980s and 1990s; this will make it less attractive to networks of suppliers. And it shows no sign of being able to match the kind of investment China has made in infrastructure that could lead to a comparable influx of investment.

China won't be the best place for everything. Some industries will remain impossible to migrate to China. For example, as long as China maintains an unconvertible currency, global financial institutions cannot conduct full-scale cross-border business from China. Telecommunications services, closed in China to foreign participation, will have natural constraints around global development. Some industries, such as the motor vehicles industry, have to maintain production locations around the world; these will continue to be based around several key production nodes in the world's largest markets. Comparative advantage will also be a factor: Chinese businesses will eschew enterprises that do not bring them sufficient returns. At the same time, many entire industries, like aircraft manufacturing, will establish a Chinese presence with dramatic speed and thus become global in a new way.

The Future of Foreign Investment

As multinationals continue to take elements of their value chain to China, foreign investment can be expected to increase. The global financial crisis may lead to a decline in the rate of investment volume in the immediate future. It might generate protectionist pressure that shows the growth of outsourcing and value-chain migration for a time. But this must not be mistaken for any fundamental alteration in the overarching trend. Indeed, it may contribute to a rise in foreign investment, as many companies will be under even greater pressure to enter China or to grow their Chinese business. They will still look to China to reduce costs, but they will also be drawn to the Chinese consumer markets, which will offer stronger growth than the "mature markets" of developed countries.

We will see a further simplifying and shortening of supply chains and a continued outsourcing of manufacturing. Chinese companies in particular will drive the commoditization of more products in many high-volume end-use segments, from laptops and computer peripherals to what were formerly high-end consumer electronics. This in turn will continue to accelerate demand for production outsourcing to the lowest-cost manufacturing centers.

Before the onset of the global financial crisis there was widespread speculation that rising costs, particularly for labor but also for other inputs, including land and materials, could lead low-cost manufacturers to favor other locations, such as Vietnam, over China. However, only some of the lowest-end manufacturers appear to be moving operations outside China. Often, manufacturers move within China, to locations farther inland. Intel, for example, is relocating some facilities from Shanghai to the inland city of Chengdu, where it had previously established a test and assembly plant. Already a network of expressways links the most important inland locations to the coast. That infrastructure will improve, thanks to the emphasis on transportation in the stimulus measures of 2008–2009.

The strengths of coastal China, especially in its key locations around the Yangtze and Pearl River deltas, will also improve over the next decade, especially for manufacturing sites a little further up the value chain. Even if costs rise, innovations in production processes (generated by the fiercely entrepreneurial will to succeed among Chinese companies) will continue to keep manufacturing competitive.

As more suppliers and manufacturers set up in China, the outsourcing and procurement trends of low-cost manufacturing will migrate to higher-end, lower-volume products such as medical equipment, machinery, automobile components, and other higher-end technologies. Other industries will include power generation, especially in areas to do with increasing energy efficiency, and electronics and IT, where ever greater numbers of Chinese manufacturers will replace manufacturers of components and modules from other countries.

The Chinese government is not likely to change its policies around strategic industry sectors, no matter how integrated its economy becomes. Thus, China will not welcome foreign investment in industries that are regarded as strategic (nor in those where it perceives its companies are not receiving reciprocal treatment overseas). In the longer run, official China is likely to modify its definition of which sectors are strategic and which not, narrowing access in some industries and opening it further in others. During the next few years, especially during the economic slowdown accompanying the global financial crisis, Chinese officials and the Chinese public may suspect other countries of protectionist or anti-Chinese sentiment. This in turn could lead the government to restrict large-scale overseas penetration of Chinese markets, by blocking foreign acquisitions of some Chinese companies. This has already happened to Coca-Cola in 2009. Seeking to own local brands, it offered $2.4 billion to buy China's largest juice maker, Huiyuan Juice. This offer was rejected by the Ministry of Commerce.

Tempting as it will be to attribute such events to the emergence of a protectionist outlook on the part of official China, they will tend to be tactical, not strategic. They will reflect a desire to protect individual companies rather than the economy as a whole. The broad thrust of maintaining China's openness to foreign investment and the arrival of value-chain elements will remain in place.

The Chinese One World Company

China will eventually produce its own one world companies. Official China has long made it clear that one of its major economic goals is to establish Chinese enterprises among the ranks of the world's leading businesses. Superficially, this process would appear to be under way. In 2009, China had thirty-four members of the Fortune Global 500.[9] China's outbound investment was more than $52 billion in 2009, having risen from $1 billion to $3 billion annually in the early 2000s.[10]

However, China still has a way to go before its companies attain the status of true one world multinationals. With one exception, all China's Fortune 500 companies are centrally controlled state-owned companies, and their bulk can be attributed to operating in protected domestic markets. The exception is SAIC, the joint venture partner to VW and GM. But it is owned by the Shanghai municipal government and for all intents and purposes has the same status as a centrally controlled state company.

Examining the size of China's outbound investment is also misleading. At least before the global financial crisis, much of Chinese spending abroad was used to either secure natural resources (most notably oil) or to buy passive stakes in overseas banks. For example, more than 60 percent of the total overseas investment in the first half of 2009 can be attributed to just four deals: Sinopec acquiring Africa's Addax Petroleum Corp for $7.1 billion; Hunan Valin Iron and Steel acquiring a 16.5 percent stake of Australia's Fortescue Metals for $1.9 billion; the full acquisition of Oz Metals in Australia by China Minmetals for $1.4 billion; and PetroChina's 45.5 percent stake in Singapore Petroleum for $1 billion.

Moreover, before Chinese companies, whether state-owned or private, start making their presence felt on a major scale, they will have to confront two major obstacles: one internal, the other external.

The internal obstacle is the transformation Chinese companies have to make in their management practices to prepare themselves for global competition. Although the internal structures of most larger enterprises are formally similar to those of Western multinationals, both the nature and depth of business knowledge in China is nowhere near the same. The rate of China's economic growth has far exceeded its capacity to educate and train people for working in a globalized economy, let alone give them the experience necessary, especially when it comes to doing business outside China's borders.

Within many private enterprises, power is overconcentrated in one figure: the owner-operator. Sometimes, this individual relies on a handful of trusted senior advisors. This form of entrepreneurship can lead to fast, dynamic decision making, but it has also contributed to a culture of opportunism. While China's economy boomed, many companies grew by moving from one hot new business area to another, often neglecting their original business along the way. Now, some companies find themselves with a portfolio of businesses spread across a group of increasingly competitive sectors and too little in-depth insight into any of them.

In state-owned companies, the leadership problem is often the opposite. Before acting, it is customary for executive teams in such companies to establish a consensus; doing so can be time consuming, making it a challenge for companies to effect rapid change. Moreover, state-owned enterprises are filled with managers with years of experience, but whose knowledge typically extends little beyond their own area of expertise. Thanks to their socialist legacy, these companies often have long histories of being process oriented and reliant on numerical measures of development. This makes fostering individual initiative hard. With older managers tending to remain in their positions for years, too many younger managers hit ceilings early in their career. Government rules make it hard to offer the incentives needed to retain and maximize the effect of talented staff. Profits, for example, can't be redistributed to managers within a state-owned company.

For both private and state-owned companies the challenge is therefore developing executive teams who can devise and implement strong, resilient, and flexible strategies.

The external obstacle is the hostility to China's reemergence as a global economic power, particularly from the United States. This first manifested itself publicly in 2005, when CNOOC, the smallest of China's three major oil companies, offered $18.5 billion to buy American oil company Unocal. Despite Unocal providing less than one percent of the United States's oil and gas needs, the bid generated a storm of opposition from American politicians and others opposing the deal as a threat to U.S. energy security. Offers by CNOOC to keep all Unocal's American energy assets in the United States were not enough, and eventually CNOOC retracted its bid.

Huawei Technologies had a similar experience in 2008 when it joined Bain Capital in a $2.2 billion bid to buy out communications equipment maker 3Com. Although Huawei would only have ended up with 16.5 percent of 3Com, the purchase was abandoned in the face of political opposition in Washington.

Elsewhere, China's expanding presence in Africa, which has become a major source of oil and other resources, has proved a source of friction, most prominently over Sudan, where China's investment in oil fields have resulted in widely reported criticism from Western human rights groups.[11] And in 2009, a bid by the state-owned Chinalco for a

$1.9 billion stake in the British-Australian mining company Rio Tinto was quashed, in part, by political opposition in Australia.[12]

To many Chinese, all these responses suggest double standards, particularly given efforts by the United States and other developed countries to acquire businesses in China and their efforts to protect their economic interests in the Middle East and elsewhere. (From this perspective, the U.S.-led invasion of Iraq was primarily an effort to preserve American oil rights.) And there are indeed reasons to suspect self-serving motives behind much of the criticism of China's overseas activities. For example, China, India, and Malaysia all have significant economic interests in Sudan's oil industry. But no other country has been subjected to the same degree of criticism as China has for activities there.

Hypocritical or not, the challenge of overcoming such responses is real. Overcoming the problems of management shortcomings and overseas hostility are long-term challenges, ones that will need at least a decade to work through.

And these obstacles will be overcome. Just as multinational companies come to China because they have no alternative, so Chinese companies will have to go overseas both to reach new markets and to maintain their competitiveness within their home markets. Moreover, both Chinese companies and official China want this sort of global expansion. It represents one more aspect of the intense economic desire that is driving the country forward.

China's Soft Power

China will achieve its overseas goals by riding the familiar forces of globalization: communications, trade, and investment. In early 2009, it was widely reported that the government was planning to spend several billion dollars developing global media, including a twenty-four-hour television station loosely based on Al Jazeera, to establish credible voices for Chinese news, analysis, and opinions.[13]

Since 2004, it has also been sponsoring the establishment of Confucius Institutes around the world: cultural centers, often based in universities or other educational institutes, that promote the teaching of Chinese languages and Chinese culture. And around the time of the G20 summit held in April 2009, China launched a series of economic proposals clearly aimed at showing it intended to play a more influential role in setting the global economic agenda.

Communications measures like this represent attempts to develop China's soft power. Political analyst Joseph Nye first coined the term *soft power* as a counterpoint to military might: national leaders, argues Nye, can gain as much from wielding diplomacy and economic incentives effectively as they can from waging war. Corporations also have a form of soft power at their disposal: instead of hostile takeovers and poaching either markets or key people, they can build alliances, cultivate markets, and provide reasons for other members of the value chain to trust them and profit from association with them.

Chinese government and corporate leaders will step up their soft power efforts in the coming decade, especially where these moves can be expected to smooth the way for international expansion of China's economic and other interests in the United States and Europe. Already, many Chinese corporate leaders know that sheer scale and financial might alone are not enough to allow them to expand internationally. They know they need to be able to influence and attract stakeholders— including customers, employees, shareholders, governments, and the broader community—in every country where they plan to operate. As with any business strategy, developing the capabilities of soft power calls for mapping out a clear path of initiatives, timelines, investments, and milestones. As implementation proceeds, plans will need to be updated and adapted, interdependencies tracked and managed, successes built upon, and shortcomings addressed. All this will require complex, cross-functional, organizationwide efforts that will demand much time and attention from senior management.

While each company needs to forge its own path, Chinese companies can learn from those who have gone before them. The success of Japanese and Korean companies illustrates the size of the prizes on offer—

consider the presence of Toyota, Sony, Toshiba, Sanyo, and Hyundai in the U.S. economy—and the routes toward winning them. Guided by these examples and bolstered by continued economic development at home, Chinese companies are finding themselves positioned to become global powers more quickly than their predecessors.

Trade will expand through the well-developed Chinese value chains. The Chinese businesses best positioned to accomplish this fall into two categories. The first group will be manufacturers and other firms that can compete with multinationals or offer goods or skills that they need, typically at very specific points on the value chains of specific industries. These include suppliers such as BYD, with its competence in batteries, or Wanxiang, which first established itself as a manufacturer of universal joints. The second group will be those that have succeeded in establishing a dominant position in a market segment within China and can use that position for global leverage. These include the personal computer maker Lenovo, the appliances manufacturer Haier, and the telecommunications operator China Mobile.

Most Chinese companies lack the capabilities they need to single-handedly expand their domestic operations into international territory. They will need international partners to improve the weaker aspects of their own value chains. Among the functional areas particularly in need of support are marketing and distribution, brand development, public relations, and IT support. Even when Chinese companies are successful with their purchases, turning them into successful, long-term businesses is not easy. In 2004, the electronic consumer goods manufacturer TCL became the world's largest television manufacturer when it paid $282 million to become the dominant partner in a joint venture with French consumer electronics company Thomson Electronics. Its strategy was straightforward: use Thomson's brand name and marketing reach to go global. The venture was a disaster, losing several hundred million dollars in its first twenty-one months of operation.

Investment will be another means by which Chinese companies reach out. This will be accelerated in the aftermath of the global economic crisis. While China's total outbound investment and acquisitions fell off sharply in the second half of 2008, it should rise again in 2009 and 2010 as Chinese companies take advantage of lower prices. Although the CNOOC-Unocal and Chinalco-Rio Tinto deals did not succeed, they demonstrate the scale at which Chinese companies will seek acquisition. These companies will tend to buy stakes for strategic reasons, such as access to resources or to lay the foundations for a long-term relationship, rather than buying companies outright with the goal of installing their own management teams to run them.

Deals on such a scale will be dominated by the big state-owned companies in the immediate future. But because state-owned companies will find their freedom constricted—both by having to tailor their needs to those of official China and being subject to suspicion because of their government ties—China's first truly one world companies are more likely to emerge from businesses now in the next tier down: the private or semiprivate businesses that are growing fast and have more freedom to act independently. Huawei Technologies is often singled out as a prime contender, although its close ties to the government, despite being privately held, have led to opposition such as that which derailed the 3Com bid. Its main competitor, ZTE, is another candidate.

Chinese companies in less strategic industries, such as the white-goods maker Haier, the automotive components firm Wanxiang, and the automaker Geely, receive less official support and have a freer hand to make their own decisions. Of these, Haier has been the most successful, establishing itself as the world's fourth-largest home appliances manufacturer. In 2008, one-third of its $17.8 billion in revenues came from outside China.

However, it is unlikely that many other such companies will emerge rapidly, especially given the lack of overseas demand expected in the next few years. The story of Lenovo provides a good example of the difficulty of this transition. As China's highest-profile manufacturer of personal computers, Lenovo has deliberately tried to be a model one world company ever since its acquisition of IBM's personal computing division in 2004. But it is still not clear whether that acquisition will ultimately be financially successful. After reporting losses of nearly $100 million in the last quarter of 2008, Lenovo ousted its American CEO and announced it would be focusing on the Chinese market. In 2009, it was still unclear whether Lenovo would evolve into a global company or retreat to being primarily a domestic one.

Instead, Chinese companies will concentrate on developing and honing their capabilities in China, both strengthening their own value chains and integrating themselves into the value chains of multinationals. Such processes are already well advanced in the automotive industry. The majority of China's cars are made in Sino-foreign joint venture plants, many of which initially used a large proportion of imported parts and systems. Only after these plants were up and running have components makers sprung up to support them. Developing this part of the automaking value chain is crucial for China's own vehicle-making brands; as in Japan, the United States, and Europe, the viability of a national automobile industry depends in large part on the robustness and quality of its network of suppliers.

In addition to developing value chains within China, some Chinese vehicle makers have tried to integrate themselves with global companies. In 2007, Chery reached a provisional agreement with Chrysler to build small cars on the American company's behalf. Although that deal was abandoned in 2008, it points the way forward to the kind of arrangement Chinese and foreign companies could be making in the future. For a business such as BYD, it may make sense to tie up with a partner in the United States to sell its new line of electric cars there, rather than embark on trying to set up a distribution and support network of its own.

Indeed, the first Chinese companies that become one world companies and enter global markets will do so by forming partnerships with foreign companies, tied into their value chains. This will not be perceived as Chinese companies—despite their Chinese government support and financial firepower—"taking over" other companies. Rather, it will be a gradual process, in which Chinese companies establish themselves, step by step, alongside other multinational businesses, just as European-, North American–, and Japanese-based multinationals have done before them. This is likely to happen with resources first, and in developing economies rather than developed ones.

The Chinese companies that make this transition will use every advantage they have, including the significant leverage of backing from official China. And though they take on one world elements, they will remain essentially Chinese, especially the strategic state-owned enterprises. For now, all of China's largest companies fall into this category. These companies can be expected to behave like "Confucian multinationals," answerable to the government, which will oversee appointments of their top officials who will continue to rotate them in and out of government. (The official who set up Chinalco's Rio Tinto offer, the company's then chairman, Xiao Yaqing, was transferred to China's cabinet, the State Council, while the deal was being scrutinized by the Australian government. This episode demonstrated how close the ties are between the government and its core group of state-owned enterprises. Any government claims to maintain an arm's-length relationship in the management of these companies should be treated with skepticism.)

Foreign governments and commentators are less likely to be suspicious of private companies, so they will face fewer external barriers to their overseas expansion, particularly in making acquisitions. Even these companies, however, are likely to maintain relatively strong ties with the Chinese government. As I noted in the previous chapter, official China remains suspicious of the emergence of any organization or individual that could form an independent locus of power and certainly doesn't want to see the emergence of oligarchs or a tycoon class. So while private companies have more freedom to go their own way and correspondingly receive less support, it is unlikely that the larger ones either will want or be able to act entirely independently of the state.

Globalization in Pursuit of Stability

China's leaders will continue to be major advocates of globalization. It offers them the tools through which their country's economy and businesses can grow, through which they can extend their reach and influence worldwide, and most of all, through which they can grow a prosperous and thus politically stable state.

They know this path will inherently involve a long, hard struggle, in which many Chinese business and political leaders will gradually acquire the skills and knowledge, especially the soft-power skills, that they need to operate globally. But beyond this lies a greater agenda. China's leaders know that economic value in the twenty-first century will be created and distributed from knowledge accessed via globalized networks of communications, technology, and investment. Their ultimate goal therefore is the creation of a knowledge-based economy.

This will require balancing the economy's needs for openness and integration with their own desires to retain political and social control. In this, they will seek to set limits on the country's engagement with the outside world. Certainly they don't see themselves as "surrendering" to the forces of globalization. They will not open China's banking system or stock markets to any major degree of foreign participation. While they have lowered the obstacles to business both at China's borders and within them, along the way introducing the "flattening" forces of instant connection, and with them both instant communication and near-instant competition, China is not a flat or borderless country. Nor will it become one.

So far, through their openness to the world, China's leaders have learned that they can increase their own ability to manage their destiny.

They have proven capable, as we saw in the last chapter, of shaping and guiding domestic public opinion. Thanks to China's scale and increasing strength, they also believe they will have a growing ability to project their own presence on the rest of the world.

International companies should be excited by the opportunities that a one world with an active and powerful China offers them. But they must always bear in mind the fact that Chinese leaders have their own agenda. However free flowing the connections and flows of goods, information, investment, and people may appear, these are all ultimately restricted. Although many multinationals will tie their future to China, and many Chinese companies will tie their futures to the rest of the world, there will remain limits on the ultimate degree of integration. Conducting business in China and with Chinese companies will remain local in its operations and interactions, and though integrated to an unprecedented degree, it will always be subject to national considerations.

The most successful one world companies will be those that negotiate the multilevel intricacies of relationships with officials, value-chain partners, and customers, then integrate these elements into a global framework. Bringing these complexities into coherent focus is the foundation of any China strategy.

CHAPTER 6

Vision

I N 2004, SHANE TEDJARATI joined Honeywell as its China president. Honeywell's lines of business—in aerospace, industrial and consumer control devices, specialty materials, and transportation systems—were expanding in China. But revenues were growing by just a few percent annually. He set about changing that.

Tedjarati describes his approach as swapping a "West to East" approach for an "East to West" one. Before, Honeywell had had a defensive attitude to the Chinese market. It saw the country as a place where it had to have a presence, but where growth would come in the future, once the country had developed a little further. Honeywell hadn't introduced its more advanced products for fear they would be counterfeited. Many foreign companies operate like this—seeing what products they have that might be appropriate for China, then selling a small volume, usually into China's top-tier markets. They postpone any further expansion, waiting for domestic markets to reach the size and sophistication where they will need the kinds of products they already sell in the West.

Instead, Tedjarati set up Honeywell to develop products in China for China, and particularly its mid- and lower-tier markets. Essentially, the company "rethought" China. Instead of viewing China as a distant outpost of its U.S.-centric operations, Honeywell looked for ways of making China a core part of its global operations, where value could be originated. The company started taking China's markets seriously on their own terms, rather than waiting for growth to come and make the Chinese economy look like that of other places.

To accomplish this, Honeywell had to follow IBM's example and move key parts of its operations to China. The Asia-Pacific headquarters for all four of its strategic business groups were relocated to Shanghai. The company opened a global engineering center in the western city of Chongqing and relocated the global headquarters of its electronic materials division from the United States to Shanghai.

Tedjarati knew what he wanted to do couldn't be done with its existing Chinese staff. It needed more local expertise—a lot more. The company more than doubled its China staff to more than 8,000 people, with a huge proportion of these new hires going to work in an entirely new 1,000-person research and development center in Shanghai.

With the right people in place, Honeywell then began developing new versions of its industrial controls and other products. Some had fewer functions. Others were simply cheaper. Others were essentially new products. The outcome: a range of Honeywell products tailored for the Chinese market, many of which could be exported for sale in other parts of the world. Though they often sold for less than Honeywell's other products, the margins on these goods weren't necessarily lower. In many cases, thanks to lower development and production costs combined with higher sales volumes, they were higher. Within four years, Honeywell's China revenues were up threefold.

As for counterfeiting, Tedjarati points out that if a company is not present in a market, other companies may copy its product to fill the gap. But while the copier's offerings may be cheaper, they are almost certainly inferior and probably cannot be properly supported. If a business enters China with a sophisticated product that requires support and services, it may be too much trouble for other companies to compete.

The Components of a Chinese Strategy

To make his strategy work, Shane Tedjarati drew on three major strengths. First, his deep China experience. He speaks Mandarin (and five other languages). Since arriving in China in 1992, he's traveled widely across the country, talking to people wherever he's been. He joined Honeywell after first building a business selling information technology to Chinese banks and then serving as the China head for Deloitte Consulting.

Second, he approached the country as a place of strategic value. He looked for opportunities to migrate a far greater part of Honeywell's global value chain to the country; he tapped into China's pools of research talent to develop new products; and he reevaluated the stage of development of its markets.

Third, he didn't isolate China from the rest of the world. Under Tedjarati, Honeywell developed a China vision that allowed it to rework its global outlook, leading to a new strategic outlook for the company. Indeed, since 2008, Tedjarati's responsibilities have been expanded to include India, with the goal of identifying the same kind of possibilities that Honeywell has found in China.

Many companies remain in Honeywell's former position. They have poured billions of dollars, yen, and euros into China, but set limited objectives. Either they seek to create a low-cost manufacturing platform to make and export products to other markets, or they want to create sales and distribution networks to reach China's consumers, sometimes with products made in China, but also with goods imported into the country. These goals may seem admirable, but they exhibit tunnel vision. They represent a narrow view of China: perhaps as purely a venue for low-cost sourcing, or as a rapidly expanding pool of customers who are attracted to imported goods, or as a country of potential, but not yet a place where real gains can be realized now.

By contrast, one world companies recognize what it means to operate on a global stage. China isn't the only country playing a role in their plans, but with its established manufacturing base and huge population rapidly growing more affluent, it is a predominant base—and a platform for developing the kinds of products and services that will sell around the world, especially to the millions of newly urbanized people joining the middle class in emerging economies. Companies like Honeywell, that take advantage of the game-changing nature of China in the global economy, are already reaping the benefits. Their examples can offer key lessons to companies that decide to follow in their footsteps.

This chapter describes the mindset of the Chinese strategist; or rather, the business strategist who recognizes that China is a key part of the global business environment. It shows how to develop a strategic vision building upon the knowledge of China (and related global trends) that was laid out in the previous chapters.

According to the classic approach to business strategy, executives are advised that they need to consider the "three Cs"—customers, competitors, and their own company. For China, another "C" needs to be added: context. Understanding China's context, how it is evolving, and how this evolution will affect the structure, conduct, and performance of a company's industry is vital.

I have built this chapter around three stages of diagnosis and decision making, each with questions for the individual reader. In the first stage, establish where your company is in relation to China's development. In the second, figure out where your company wants to go. In the third, anticipate what might happen along the way, and put yourself in a position to be ready for possible threats and opportunities. To further help companies with this process, the chapter closes with a list of the key steps necessary to become a one world company.

But let's start with a word of warning. Be careful about applying a traditional, static long-term planning approach. Things can change very rapidly in China. Straightforward extrapolations of any state of affairs are highly reliable guides. The solution to this dilemma is to build your own capabilities and understanding: to think in terms of understanding China's business context and the forces that drive change in the country rather than moving toward a fixed set of targets. That is why I have spent so much time in the previous chapters exploring the motivations of China's companies, leaders, and consumers.

The best companies operating in China have built up this knowledge in-house by taking on executives who have a deep experience and understanding of the country. These include people such as KFC's Sam Su, Honeywell's Shane Tedjarati, and Tetra Pak's Hudson Lee. Bringing such expertise on board, as KFC, Honeywell, and Tetra Pak did, is the single most important step any company can make.

These companies also balance their in-county expertise with a grasp of the wider picture. They have experienced global executives on hand who are neither dismissive of China nor China-centric. They possess in-depth knowledge of the country, *and* knowledge of global business. Ingrained, experience-based judgment about both domains is a prerequisite to integrating a successful China operation into a company's worldwide structure. And that, in turn, can transform a global company's performance.

Where You Are

To figure out where to start, begin with two questions aimed at delineating your company's current position and its potential to migrate elements of its value chain to China.

1. What's your location on the product market freedom matrix?

In chapter 2, I used the "product market freedom matrix" framework to depict the general differentiation of industries in China. Now, it is time to apply it to your own situation (see exhibit 6-1). If there is one thing that determines what a company may or may not be able to achieve in China, it is the position of its industry on the product market freedom matrix and the degree to which that position is changing. This indicates the degree to which a company can expect to operate without official hindrance and the type and extent of competition present. Companies

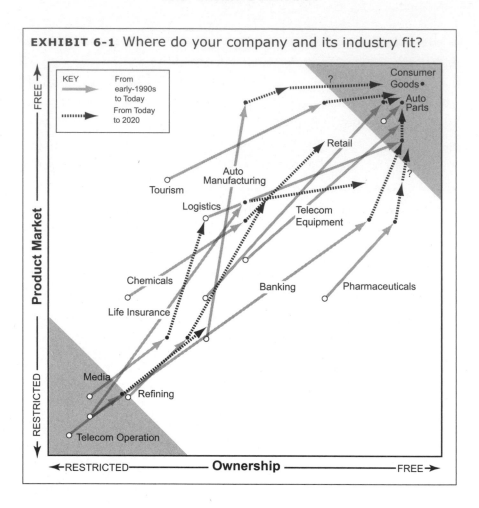

EXHIBIT 6-1 Where do your company and its industry fit?

then need to establish the official pressures determining the extent to which a sector is being liberalized and at what rate change is taking place.

Be aware of the limits of the table. It is not absolute, and the realities of any sector can be surprisingly complex. Very few sectors remain totally off-limits to foreign involvement. Even in those that are, many multinationals have hopes that at some point they will be liberalized and entrance allowed to overseas companies. And the trajectory of product market freedom can also change. Although liberalization of industries remains the general trend, it is not inevitable, and there can be significant variations over time.

In the early to mid-1990s, for example, many of the world's leading telecom operators established some kind of presence in China. They all hoped to gain entry when telecom services were liberalized. That has yet to happen: the industry remains 100 percent in the hands of state-owned companies. It will almost certainly remain that way. Consequently, almost all of the operators from around the world have packed their bags and left. But as we saw in chapter 4, the bar on operators hasn't precluded some foreign telecom equipment makers from establishing a major and hugely profitable presence in the country. Along the way, they helped the country's operators to build their networks and equipment makers to acquire the technology and know-how needed to establish themselves as major businesses; this created a new and longstanding set of customer relationships.

Other industries have complex rules for foreign ownership. For example, non-Chinese vehicle makers are restricted to a maximum stake of 50 percent in any single operation. In the banking sector, as we saw in chapter 4, foreign banks can operate their own 100-percent-owned operations, but can only own up to 20 percent of a Chinese bank.

Even in industries that are almost totally open to foreign involvement, appreciating when "Official China" may become involved is a vital skill. The soft drinks sector has long been open to companies from any country, with almost no oversight from the government. However, as noted in chapter 5, when Coca-Cola attempted to buy China's biggest juice maker, Huiyuan Juice, in 2008, it ran into official resistance. The Ministry of Commerce eventually rejected the bid in 2009, citing its likely effect on reducing competition.

In short, while the Chinese government has generally moved toward liberalizing its industry sectors, there is no single model of liberalization. Different sectors are moving in slightly different directions at different rates. Establishing a company's position on the product market freedom matrix establishes a broad context, then allows you to plot the nature of the specific constraints in play in your specific sector.

This will have a significant effect on your competitive strategy. Companies engaging in the most restricted industries may need to resort to "positioning" or building connections with well-placed officials (or *guanxi,* as they are known in Chinese) as their major source of competitive advantage. For example, during most of the 1990s, foreign insurance companies anticipated the opening of the Chinese market. With hopes of winning licenses from the Chinese government, they set up offices in Beijing to build and maintain *guanxi* with government officials. On the other hand, those in the most deregulated industries will typically find themselves competing in one of the fiercest, no-holds-barred markets anywhere, with competitors from all over the world striving to get a piece of the action. Companies in these sectors will do better relying on strong capabilities, not connections. At the same time, even in the most open industries with a large number of competing businesses, the government will continue to watch over what is going on and intervene whenever it deems necessary. And the larger your company, and the more strategic its industry, the more likely you are to encounter such official intervention. In such an environment, there are no clear rules, but there are great opportunities.

2. What possibilities exist for your company to migrate a far greater share of its value chain into China?

This question prompts you to stop thinking of China as a stand-alone location "out there" and instead to treat it as a place with advanced capabilities. In particular, it asks you to consider moving some key elements of your business into China now, including core practices previously maintained at headquarters or in other parts of the world.

As I noted in chapter 3, tapping into China's research and development skills is one area of rich potential for many companies, either on their own or in partnership with Chinese firms or research institutes. Information technology companies such as IBM have been in the vanguard, but others are following, in industries including consumer products, pharmaceuticals, motor vehicles, chemicals, materials, and transportation. So far, many of these facilities conduct little genuine research; their main focus is product localization and testing. But establishing them allows a company to position itself to tap into the most advanced research being done in China, especially in industries the government is prioritizing, such as aerospace and communications technology. By first becoming aware of the country's research potential firsthand, these companies can then hire talent more effectively in what is already a very competitive market.

Some companies are moving much of their operations to China. Samsung decided to invest $1 billion this way in 2009 to develop more low- to mid-tier products and give itself broader market coverage. Siemens announced in 2009 that it would add $208 million, targeted specifically at alternative energy, on top of its existing $1.4 billion of general investment. Nike is investing some $100 million to build its largest logistics center in Asia in the eastern province of Jiangsu.

Other companies are starting to explore the possibilities that developments in supply-chain services offer, particularly in the trading regions of southern and eastern China. Aside from IBM, a handful of major businesses operate major procurement operations in Shenzhen, most notably Wal-Mart, which sources around $30 billion worth of goods from China each year.

On the marketing and sales side, the great challenge will be integrating the differing needs of different parts of China into an overall whole, ensuring that the right goods are being produced for each different segment, and that as markets evolve they are supplied with the right mix of products. As you will see shortly, the complexities arising in reaching new tiers of Chinese consumers will call for bringing your best practices to China, not to assume—as you may have assumed about other emerging markets—that you can get by there with cruder approaches. And at the same time, you will have to ascertain whether goods produced in China for China are suitable for sale in other markets around the world, embracing Shane Tedjarati's "East to West" approach.

Where You Want to Go

The next step in building a China strategy is to set out the path for creating a one world enterprise. The next two questions are designed to help establish fundamental guiding principles for organizing your company's China operations and integrating your China strategy with those of your other businesses around the world.

3. How can China's strengths be integrated into your company's global value chain outside China?

Many multinational companies, either through superficial planning for China or by treating the country in isolation from their other plans, suboptimize around narrow objectives. While driving their China-sourcing programs, for example, procurement managers are usually well aligned with the objectives of manufacturing, logistics, and quality assurance. However, in many companies they fail to work with sales and marketing teams to consider how the total benefits of a presence in China could best help their companies. In other companies, distracted by the promise of selling to potentially hundreds of millions of customers, marketing and sales managers fail to consider how the volume a major sales success in China would create could affect their companies' global sourcing practices and manufacturing operations.

The most globally successful companies—IBM, Honeywell, and General Electric among them—see China in a global context, as part of an international web of capabilities, including manufacturing, innovation, new business model incubation, and talent development. The leaders of these companies do not think of China as a stand-alone country, but as a part of their global supply chain and overall business. One specific example: In 2009, as it restructured, GM moved its international headquarters to Shanghai and not to Europe, Japan, or elsewhere.

A growing number of companies recognize the value of this sort of one world strategy. A study of manufacturing competitiveness conducted jointly in 2007–2008 by the American Chamber of Commerce in

Shanghai (AmCham) and Booz & Company found that only a quarter of the survey respondents exhibited the characteristics of a globally integrated company, while half still leveraged only the sourcing operation or the sales operation, and a quarter are hardly in the game of global integration at all. That same year, only 47 percent of the respondents said that their motives for setting up manufacturing bases in China included both cost savings and access to the local sales market. But in 2009, that number rose to 57 percent, and there was a corresponding rise in the number of companies demonstrating global integration in practice, nor have they integrated their export manufacturing operations with their efforts to reach China's markets. The studies have also found that those who combine their China market and export-oriented operations perform substantially better, with much higher average profit margins (30 percent versus 18 percent in 2008) and an EBIT level on average 8 percent higher.[1]

Fortunately, changes taking place in China's business environment provide an opportunity to leap ahead. Up to now, manufacturing multinationals have tended to build export-oriented factories with abundant, cheap labor and using low levels of technology, assuming that any problems would be offset by the low costs associated with operating in China. This is changing. Due to rising costs, particularly for labor, but also materials, and an appreciation in value of China's currency, the yuan, against the dollar, both the sourcing and sales models used by many companies in China are coming under pressure. (Although the appreciation of the yuan halted in the second half of 2008, largely due to the effects of the global financial crisis, the long-term trend is likely to be a continued gradual rise in value of the yuan against other major currencies.) There will consequently be more of both an imperative and a means to integrate Chinese operations with those in the rest of the world.

The specific moves to make depend on an in-depth diagnosis of the relationship between your company's strengths in China and its global strengths. For example:

- Where is China relative to your global industry life cycle? How fast will it evolve and in what direction?
- How important is global integration for your China business now? How important will it be in the future?
- What will be the impact to your global competitive position if China cannot be integrated into your global business systems?
- What steps can you take to ensure that integration will be properly designed and executed?
- Who will be overseeing this integration?

All of these diagnostics should be the subject of continuing in-depth discussion between headquarters and China operations. Indeed, a key element in executing your strategy will be the maintenance and management of communications between China operations and global headquarters. Keeping headquarters informed of what's happening in China can be a challenge, but when it is overlooked, then headquarters executives often fail to understand fully the underlying factors driving developments in China. Paying attention to this relationship is vital. Without good communication, headquarters may find it difficult to react to possibilities and opportunities rapidly enough, and you may even find your burgeoning business in China causing disruptions in other parts of the enterprise thousands of miles away, and with apparently only indirect links to the country. Thus one final subquestion must be addressed:

- How well equipped is your company to manage the relationship between your businesses in China and those in the rest of the world?

A related common error is to let your Chinese businesses operate without benefit of your corporation's overall knowledge base. Very few multinationals have yet imported the best practices of their operations elsewhere in the world; but as we have seen in earlier chapters, there is good reason to do so.

4. What business models commensurate with China's economic evolution should your company adopt?

If companies don't grasp the scope of what is and is not possible in China, they cannot transform their global vision into successful on-the-ground operations in the country. In my experience, the business models of multinational companies fall into one of four categories (see exhibit 6-2):

Type A: Laggards. These companies have neither established China as a low-cost country for sourcing nor entered to pursue sales opportunities. They could benefit from both sales and sourcing opportunities in China, but have not yet gotten around to doing so.

Type B: Sourcing-centric companies. These have well-established China supply bases, but they are primarily designed for export. Their sales operations and capabilities in China are limited or may be nonexistent. Those that have a small sales operation may source in China, complete production in their home country, and then reimport to China. (This approach represents a model of inefficiency.) Companies in this segment include a number of European and American producers of high-end consumer electronics and mobile-communications equipment.

Type C: Sales-centric companies. These have successfully entered the Chinese market, in some cases recording significant sales volumes, but they serve China from home-country operations or small manufacturing operations in China. These companies do not include major exports from China into their global operations. Some of the top-branded European automobile manufacturers fall into this category.

Type D: Global integrators. These companies have integrated their worldwide value and supply chains. They have brought together China sourcing, manufacturing, and selling activities, in addition to innovation activities, and these are integrated, optimized,

EXHIBIT 6-2 Business models of multinational companies in China

Source: Booz & Company

and leveraged globally. This is an elite class of companies. Many of its members are smaller or medium-sized companies that, by necessity, had to take an integrated approach early, launching a series of companywide initiatives that the boards of larger organizations might consider risky. Others started out as type B or type C companies, then graduated to an integrated approach. They tend to have a higher level of management capability, especially in understanding and exploiting the opportunities presented by moving major parts of their value chains to China, and they tend to have the resources necessary to act on opportunities much earlier.

Global integrators tend to be adept at transforming their Chinese operations into hubs for their global value chains. They thus make use of China's dual role, as discussed in earlier chapters: a key sales market and a hub for exporting products. They use their Chinese expansion to significantly improve their global economies of scale and their leverage in sourcing; and as they develop their export business from China, they gain competitive advantage by applying superior product designs and standards from elsewhere to the Chinese market.

One globally integrated company is Hansgrohe, a German plumbing products manufacturer that became part of U.S.-based Masco Corporation in 2002. This company operates a dual-mode operation from its base in Shanghai, supporting sales in dozens of cities in China and supplying its global operations network with China-made products that are exported to other countries. The company still imports some high-end products into China, but only when it makes sense. The basic products produced in China are labor intensive, whereas the premium, capital-intensive products from Germany would benefit little from China's factor-cost advantages.

Another such company is A.O. Smith, the American water heater manufacturer. In the past decade, this manufacturer has built up a management team in China and a sales network that spans across the nation. A.O. Smith has also leveraged its China market experience and production capacity to develop other overseas markets. For example, some water heater designs in China are now being brought back as "new products" to the U.S. market, strengthening the company's competitiveness in some American market segments. Some of the capacity in China was also used for exporting water heaters to India. Taking advantage of China's duality has given A.O. Smith China sales in 2007 that were six times its sales in 2001, representing a CAGR (compound annual growth rate) of over 33 percent. Moreover, A.O. Smith leads all foreign brands in Chinese market share for water heaters; it is second only to the local home appliance giant Haier.

Some very sophisticated global integrators are integrating more of their upstream activities, such as R&D and product development, into their China value chains. These include well-known consumer products companies such as Coca-Cola and P&G, which are making conscious efforts in R&D activities targeted at the local market. Many of their local products, such as Minute Maid with orange pulp, are effective combinations of local consumer insights and their global brands and platforms. Another example is Sanofi Aventis, a leading pharmaceutical company, which announced in 2008 its plan to expand the company's R&D facility in Shanghai, open a new state-of-the-art biometrics center in Beijing, and strengthen its cooperation with the Chinese Academy of Sciences. All these initiatives are expected to improve the company's capabilities and efficiency for programs ranging from new drug development to late-stage clinical studies.

As you move toward global integration, your current business model represents your starting point. But what business model—sourcing-centric, sales-centric, or global integrator—do you now hope to adopt? Decision makers trying to answer this question should consider three aspects of the country simultaneously:

First, how much of the value chain to move to China. As we have seen, the traditional view of China as a low-cost hub for sourcing and manufacturing bears very little resemblance to what China is today.

Second, how much to sell, and to whom. We have also seen how China's markets are a complex mosaic of fragmented elements, divided by geography, culture, income, education, skills, and other factors, further complicated by the rate of change they are all undergoing. For a global company to succeed in China, it will have to know the country intimately.

And third, how much to integrate globally. Deciding how far to go down the route of centering your worldwide integration around China calls for figuring out which bits of the local can be accommodated into a global framework, but doing so in a country that is very much a work in progress, with change and discontinuity the one constant.

Many global integrators, especially those looking to sell a range of goods in China, could end up running two or three of these business models simultaneously. Some product lines will be aimed at capturing the local market; these will have to be differentiated between those aimed at the more developed cities of the coast and the poorer but far more numerous third- and fourth-tier locations dispersed across much of the rest of the country. Other operations will produce higher-end goods for the developed world and China's wealthiest markets.

One common error is to avoid the lower-tier inexpensive markets. This runs the risk that Chinese companies will establish themselves there, with an eye to building positions from which they can move up to the middle tier. Such an approach also ignores the possibility of missing the revenues from the lower tiers—which, as Honeywell has shown, can be substantial. In addition, producing lower-cost alternatives to those offered by Chinese companies allows a company to tap into the same sources of value that Chinese rivals are using to establish themselves.

What Might Happen Along the Way

With this next group of five questions, corporate leaders can consider some likely scenarios for challenges and opportunities. The critical goal, during your first few years, is to build local knowledge and experience—enough to anticipate changes in the market, to resolve the various trade-offs that are the inevitable part of doing business in China, and to judge when enough data and information has been gathered to make a decision.

5. How can your company acquire the local knowledge necessary to assess China's geographical markets and their tiers?

The markets of most companies now active in China are concentrated in the three core areas described in chapter 2: the Yangtze River Delta region around Shanghai, the region around Beijing and its neighbor Tianjin, and the Pearl River Delta region running from Hong Kong to Guangzhou. In the next decades, companies that see themselves as wanting to reach the entire Chinese market will have to go much farther, multiplying their local knowledge base many times over.

This will take time. KFC, as we have seen, took nearly a decade establishing its first 100 restaurants, but then was able to add more than 2,000 after that using the knowledge it had gained in its early years. Coca-Cola and Pepsi are still putting together their knowledge bases on China's millions of retail outlets.

Knowledge can be acquired in various ways. It can be bought from various of the host of sectoral consultancies, Chinese and foreign, that have established themselves. The government has a growing body of data that is rapidly improving both in scope and reliability. The National Bureau of Statistics, its main agency responsible for collecting and collating economic and other data, has a long history of collaboration with organizations from overseas aimed at strengthening its practices and methodologies. Local companies can also be a rich source of market understanding in the regions where they operate.

Most useful, however, is the knowledge acquired through experience, the kind that comes from building out an operation product by product, city by city, province by province. Procter & Gamble has excelled with this approach, taking its personal-care range item by item across China. The French supermarket chain Carrefour has concentrated on getting the nuances of each of its stores right for the region where it operates by allowing local managers considerable latitude to source their own supplies and run their stores as they see fit. Although this model of decentralization has worked well overall, it has apparently led to the company facing problems with corruption, counterfeit goods, and health and quality standards. A company with Carrefour's strategy can succeed by learning from these experiences and codifying practices to counter them.[2]

6. How can your company's executives acquire on-the-ground experience they will need for their work?

As we have seen, many companies that have performed well in China have had their operations run by people who have worked in the country for years. They do not rotate in executives who don't understand the local context.

This has several major implications for multinational companies. Think carefully about the role of expatriates and how long they will be required in China—and on the other side of the coin, whether localization can be usefully accelerated. Whether they are local or expat, gaining the necessary experience can take several years. The ability to read and speak Chinese is highly desirable. So is global awareness; promoting executives simply because they are Chinese is not an effective way forward.

While *guanxi* are becoming less important than they were, building value-adding, mutually beneficial relationships with local partners continues to be of vital importance. It allows companies to fine-tune their understanding of developments in their industry. Connections are usually personal rather than connected to someone's position, another reason for keeping successful executives in place rather than moving them on. But note that these relationships can be subject to disruption. A central government decision can reverse years of relationship building or undertakings made by local officials.

One way of building strong ties with local businesspeople and officials is to get on the board of a Chinese company. Some of the largest domestic corporations have outsiders on their boards. For example, John Thornton, a former president of Goldman Sachs, serves on the boards of both China Netcom, one of the country's big-four telecom operators, and ICBC, the largest of its big-four banks. I am a board member of Baosteel, China's largest iron and steel group, and of the SAIC Group.

Another way to foster links is to work with the Chinese government by helping it build competency. Major global accountancy firms have advised officials on ways to structure China's tax framework; investment banks have worked with its stock exchanges, and many standards are adopted from foreign versions. Of course, there's no guarantee that the government will follow any suggestions or advice proffered, but in general officials always want to know how things are done elsewhere to see if there are measures that can be usefully introduced in China.

7. How can your company gain the ability to anticipate market discontinuities and disruptions?

Monitoring changes in the consumer markets of China is tricky enough, given China's size and the rapidly shifting demographic makeup of its cities and regions. Making matters far more complex is the government's impact on market discontinuities. Officials may decide to allow or ban a good or service, and can create and destroy markets all but overnight. In chapter 2 we saw how allowing companies to offer auto finance contributed to exponential growth in passenger car sales and how letting people buy their homes from their companies created a home mortgage market. Similarly, in mid-2008, the government actively discouraged outside companies from entering resource-intensive or pollution-heavy sectors and removed tax rebates for many categories of exports. Although various of these measures were reversed or relaxed as the economy slowed in late 2008 and early 2009, officials are likely to use such measures again in the future to guide companies away from sectors they disfavor.

Anticipating such changes is not easy. Acknowledging that they will happen, however, is essential, as then a company can be ready to move quickly when events move in its favor. For some industries, this means maintaining an office in Beijing that can liaise with the relevant ministry or other official body. But beyond this it requires a strong grasp of official China's strategic agenda and the possibilities of change; and it means having access to the best possible sources of information on government thinking.

Executives whose experience before coming to China was focused on the cost side of their businesses, as is often the case in more mature markets, may have particular difficulties in adjusting to the country's discontinuities. Revenues of businesses in developed markets are often flat or growing at a single digit rate, resulting in mindsets that tend to be attuned to linear and incremental change. China-based enterprises need managers who can see things in nonlinear fashion and then act boldly when required to do so.

8. Can your company handle the trade-offs necessary to do business in China?

Trade-offs are an essential part of doing business in China and must be accepted as such. The biggest trade-off that will present itself to almost any company is certainty versus opportunity. Given China's rate of change, the undeveloped state of many aspects of business, and short-ages of data, it is almost impossible to make decisions with the full range of knowledge most companies would like. Delaying too long may lead to a company missing out on a growth surge for its products, but moving too quickly may result in wasted investment.

Chinese companies are particularly proficient at handling such trade-offs. They pursue opportunities wherever they see them and are accustomed to rapid entry into hot new business sectors. Those that are successful with this approach can grow very fast, but they can also crash. Despite China's brief corporate history, hosts of companies have already had time to rise fast and then fall to a fraction of their former size, or even to vanish without a trace. One example is D'Long, a conglomerate that in the mid-2000s had revenues of close to $4 billion but collapsed into bankruptcy after its founder, Tang Wanxin, was found to have illegally raised capital and manipulated the share prices of various D'Long subsidiaries. He was sentenced to eight years' imprisonment. Another example is Guangdong Kelon, once one of China's leading refrigerator makers, whose chairman, Gu Chujun, was tried for embezzlement and fraud after the company overstated its revenues by $150 million and its profits by around $50 million between 2002 and 2004. Then there is Ningbo Bird, a maker of mobile phones that briefly in the early 2000s soared to become China's largest domestic mobile-phone brand, third in sales only behind Nokia and Samsung. Now it is just another of the many tens of local handset makers struggling to cope with competition from Nokia, Motorola, and Samsung.[3]

For multinationals, the trade-offs can be more nuanced. Especially in their early ventures, it is often worth trading investment for experience. Many multinationals, particularly Japanese ones, treated the 1990s and early 2000s as learning years, positioning themselves to be ready for when the economy had reached a size where they could start making serious returns. Toyota epitomized such an approach: for a long time it was widely regarded as moving too slowly, as first VW and then GM established joint ventures with the heavyweights of China's auto industry, Shanghai Automotive Industry Corporation and First Auto Works (FAW). Toyota also has a joint venture with FAW, but what could prove the jewel in its China crown is its south China operation with Guangzhou Auto, a relatively lightweight company. Based in a zone that includes a purpose-built shipping port for transporting cars to other cities along the Chinese coats, Toyota has emerged with far greater control and with a far less ambitious partner than GM and Volkswagen have. This will probably give Toyota greater control over the direction of its development, providing it can navigate the downturn in its China market share that accompanied the global economic crisis.

Many overseas businesses have been as opportunistic as their Chinese counterparts. The foreign financial institutions that took stakes in Bank of China, China Construction Bank, and Industrial and Commercial Bank of China ahead of their international listings in 2005 and 2006 accepted that although their investments weren't bringing them a say in how these banks were run, being involved early in their development appeared to be a trade-off worth making.

In many other industries, most companies wanting access to China's markets have had to trade some of their know-how and expertise in return. Siemens and Alcatel gained their footholds in the country's telecom equipment sector this way in the 1980s and 1990s. The practice also lies behind most of the large automotive joint ventures. In all such negotiations, China's greatest strength is its awareness of where it is headed: reestablishing itself as a major economic force. For this it is prepared to trade off short-term gains, particularly in market share, for longer-term access to technology and know-how.

Companies must also bear this in mind when it comes to their intellectual property. Given China's reputation for piracy and counterfeiting, there is every reason to take threats to a company's proprietary knowledge seriously. Protection measures can include keeping a key process offshore or simply ensuring that security within plants is a priority, with strict control over who is allowed to have access to which part of a factory. The trade-offs in deciding whether to transfer technologies often involve more than a simple fear of whether they will be stolen or copied. In some instances, for example, not transferring a product or a technology can be an invitation for a domestic company to try to reverse-engineer and produce their own version. Whatever the quality of their offerings may be, they know they will gain expertise in manufacturing and selling this good. Importing the good or technology, however, will make copycats vulnerable to competition from the real thing, which is usually superior and can be offered with better support. Moreover, once in the market, a company can start looking at how best to both shape it for Chinese needs and take advantage of China's lower-cost manufacturing to make its offerings more competitive.

9. Can you and your managers accept that in China it is far better to be approximately right than precisely wrong?

China will remain a not entirely transparent place to operate in for many years to come. Companies looking for certainty in this environment will find themselves foregoing action until it is too late. The country has produced a generation of executives who thrive under these conditions: figures such as Zhang Ruimin, head of Haier, or Ren Zhengfei, the founder of Huawei, know that they won't succeed by getting things right all the time. Instead, to maximize their chances of success, they are ready to take advantage of sudden openings. They act fast and decisively, anticipating possible opportunities for success rather than looking to consolidate or protect market gains already made.

A long list of multinational companies have failed because they haven't been able (or willing) to move opportunistically. Peugeot's initial venture in Guangzhou was a disaster. But many companies have learned from these experiences. Peugeot Citroën has since developed a strong joint venture in the central city of Wuhan with Dongfeng Auto, with a factory capable of producing nearly half a million cars annually.

Overall, according to the various surveys undertaken each year, profitability is rising for global companies in China. For example, the American chambers of commerce in Beijing and Shanghai found in 2008 that around three-quarters of the companies surveyed report themselves to be making money in China, a percentage that has steadily risen over the years.[4] Even more noteworthy is the fact that a decade ago, only 13 percent of companies reported margins in China higher than their worldwide averages; in mid-2008 (admittedly before the onset of the global financial crisis) this figure was approaching half.[5]

Five years ago, it was possible to make a strong case that the unknowns about China made delaying a decision to invest worthwhile. But the country is more accessible and transparent now; it is no longer excusable to claim to be operating in the dark. There are also a lot more people with experience of operating in China, Chinese as well as foreigners, and the quality of decisions is improving. The decision about how to be involved can be right or wrong; the decision not to be involved is almost certainly wrong.

Making the Transition to Being a
One World Company

Of course, not all companies need to have globally integrated, one world operations. Companies in industries such as restaurant chains, or businesses whose products and supporting services are highly tailored to particular markets, may do very well remaining local. But for those that can manage it, the benefits of being a one world company are likely to be substantial.

For companies already sourcing or manufacturing for export out of China (type B companies), the primary goal should be to gain additional scale benefits by capturing sales opportunities in the Chinese market. The key success factor is adding on-the-ground knowledge of markets to already existing relationships with local suppliers and developing the logistics and distribution skills to serve locations across the country. Wal-Mart has taken this route. Its sales from stores in China represent a total value far less than the $30 billion of goods it sources in the country. But it is expanding its footprint rapidly and using its sourcing knowledge to secure products for its stores in China.

For companies that have high volumes of sales but limited production capacity in China (type C companies), the main objective must be to take full advantage of China as a low-cost country to feed their global delivery networks. The key success factors in this case are expanding the manufacturing end of the value chain, including adding the capacity to develop products suitable for China and ensuring the right location is chosen to be able to tap into established or emerging supply networks.

Many of the global luxury vehicle manufacturers, pushed by local content rules and pulled by rapid sales growth with increasingly affluent consumers, are undergoing this process. BMW and Mercedes-Benz both have aggressive expansion plans for China, simultaneously increasing the amount of production they are conducting by localizing inputs and growing their sales networks.

Those that now have neither major sourcing nor sales operations in China have the advantage that they can build integrated operations from the start, but the disadvantage that they are likely to lack experience. They should not, however, feel that they have necessarily missed the boat; China, despite its achievements, remains at an early enough stage of its development.

Additionally, there are other important differences in the management approach, especially for aspiring one world companies. VW's experience in China illustrates this point. The German carmaker was an early entrant into China in 1984, with a great deal of success in the market due in part to its advantage as one of the first movers in the industry. It succeeded in localizing production, as well as most sourcing, and brought in a dedicated management team knowledgeable about the country. However, it was slow to react to increasing global product convergence, fueled by global mergers and acquisitions in the auto sector, and the resultant opportunity to globalize its supply base. As a result, VW continued to sell aging products while competitors introduced attractive, new vehicles with more modern technology. Between 2000 and 2006, its market share fell dramatically. At the same time, due to the lack of integration among its sales, sourcing, and production operations, VW failed to take advantage of China's low-cost sourcing base for vehicles produced in Europe.

Faced with this sharp erosion of its business, Volkswagen embarked on a five-year restructuring program. This aimed at reducing costs by increasing local sourcing and centralized purchasing for both China and global factories; better meeting customer needs with around a dozen new or upgraded models; setting up a Skoda plant (taking advantage of its lower-cost Eastern European subsidiary to make cars for the low-end of the market); and opening new dealerships, each with far more narrowly defined customer segments. By 2008, its turnaround was working, with sales increasing and its market share once again rising.[6] Though it has lost much ground to GM, Toyota, and various Chinese companies, Volkswagen is now on a path to becoming globally integrated.

A recent addition to the growing list of one world companies in China is Goodyear, which now produces some of its most advanced automobile and truck tires in China for the domestic and overseas markets. Goodyear has had a presence in China since 1994. But between 1995 and 2002, its global sales stagnated, with a compound annual growth rate of less than 1 percent. Then it made a massive investment in the northeastern coastal city of Dalian in 2002, setting up China both as an important growth engine for sales and a global supply base. To accelerate its growth, the company built a network of franchised after-market outlets to sell both its tires and other products and services related to auto servicing. From fewer than 100 outlets a few years ago, the total has grown to around 1,000 franchises. This large domestic network provides the local reach to exploit the full potential of the dual sourcing-sales mission Goodyear had originally envisaged.

Goodyear designed its strategy to take advantage of China's opportunities as both a manufacturing location and market. And it grew its sales network far faster than its main international rival, France's Michelin. Goodyear also increased its average revenue per store by 30 percent a year as it reacted to the increasingly sophisticated needs of its customers. It upgraded its outlets to offer full and tailored tire services that created additional revenue streams beyond just capturing volume growth.

Quality has been an issue for companies sourcing and exporting from China, as many domestic suppliers still do not consistently adhere to agreed standards. Goodyear's answer to this challenge was to develop long-term partnerships with its suppliers, and sometimes suppliers of suppliers, to help them reach its standards. Thanks to these measures, Goodyear's Dalian facility is now capable of producing high-end, high-value tires that have received the company's top quality rating in its global audits. And it maintains high-quality manufacturing practices

EXHIBIT 6-3 Key Elements of a China-Based One World Business

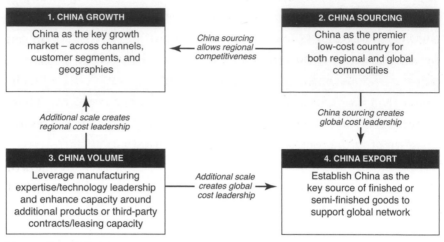

Source: Booz & Company

across its network of partners by strictly enforcing process controls and regular audits of both its own operations and those of its suppliers.

Finally, Goodyear has directly addressed the complexity of logistics for global supply networks in China. The company continually explores alternative ways of reducing lead times and costs, including using railways instead of roads to move goods. This approach demonstrates that strengthening logistics capabilities can be the single best way of improving companies' performance in the country.[7]

Whichever point they start from, the essence of what is needed to operate as a one world business is captured in exhibit 6-3. Growth in China—selling to its markets—will necessarily lead to increased China sourcing; increased China volumes in turn drive increased China exports. In many respects, the starting point is relatively unimportant; the most critical factor is the ability to use the first forms of success to drive expansion into others, and to coordinate all this with a company's global operations.

Even companies that successfully integrate their sales and sourcing operations will still have challenges ahead of them. For example, one common challenge is building sufficient scale for effective global supply-chain integration. Thus, whenever the Wanxiang Group, a major Chinese auto parts manufacturer, enters a new market around the world, it first looks for ways in which third-party distribution can broaden its reach within the shortest possible time. External partnerships are collaborative and focused on acquiring the talent and technology conducive to scale efficiency and volume enhancement. These combined efforts have been instrumental to Wanxiang's impressive sales growth of more than 30 percent since 1999.

In chapter 7, we look at the temperament and insights of leaders of the most effective companies operating in China, and the quality of versatility that allows them to succeed.

CHAPTER 7

Versatility

T o see how a versatile Chinese company responds to the challenges of its rapidly changing business environment, consider BYD, the battery and automobile manufacturer based in Shenzhen. Like many of China's most successful firms, it was founded in the mid-1990s, when Wang Chuanfu—along with hundreds of thousands of other Chinese people—abandoned his job in a state-owned enterprise to *xia hai,* or "jump into the sea" of business. Wang built the company, whose name stands for "build your dream," into one of the world's leading makers of rechargeable batteries, with an annual turnover of more than $3 billion. Its batteries turn up in around 30 percent of the world's mobile phones, three-quarters of its cordless phones, and a huge range of other tools and battery-powered goods. From batteries BYD has moved on to making additional mobile-phone components for Nokia, Motorola, and other handset makers. And it's started building cars, launching its first vehicle in 2005, a gasoline-powered sedan called the BYD F3.

At the time, many observers were suspicious. Why on earth was an electronics company moving into the auto business? Their concerns weren't alleviated when Wang in 2007 announced that his target was to make his company the world's largest carmaker, with sales of 8 or 9 million vehicles a year by 2025. That year, BYD sold 90,000 cars.

Hubris? Possibly, especially if one judged by that first gasoline-powered sedan. But the F3 represented little more than a milestone along the way to the company's real target: a battery-powered electric car. In 2008, BYD's vehicle sales rose to 170,000.[1] At the end of that year, it started selling a plug-in hybrid gasoline-electric car in China, the first such commercial model to go on sale in the world. In 2009, it was due to start selling its first all-electric car: the E6 ("E" stands for electricity). Total sales for the year are expected to be around 350,000. And backing for its project is coming from some powerful sources. In September 2008, MidAmerican Energy Holdings Co., an Iowa-based energy producer majority owned by Warren Buffett's Berkshire Hathaway, bought 10 percent of the company for $230 million.[2]

If all of this makes BYD seem unusually flexible for an automotive company, that's not surprising; it has long been noted for its ability to adapt. It established itself by displacing the Japanese companies that dominated the battery industry in the mid-1990s. Where these companies were focused on improving the quality and capabilities of their products, which made them expensive, BYD set out make the same kind of batteries but at a much, much cheaper price point. Using low-cost labor instead of expensive automated production lines, and looking wherever possible to find alternative cheaper materials, it ended up with batteries that cost a fraction of their Japanese-made equivalents. It used its lower unit cost to build economies of scale, which in turn allowed it to extend its market from mobile phones and other high-end products to cheap consumer goods such as toys.

The outcome is a company with a huge workforce: around 130,000 people, mostly young women who work manually on production lines, but including an army of 10,000 R&D staff continually modifying and improving BYD's products, production techniques, and material inputs.

On the foundations he has already built, Wang, still only in his early forties, may well be able to transform the world of carmaking. If he succeeds, it will be in an industry notorious for its daunting barriers to entry. And yet the BYD vision stands out, even among that of most other successful entrepreneurs in China, because of the way in which it dovetails with three of official China's aspirations: to make the automotive sector one of China's pillar industries; to establish China as a leading source of innovation, particularly in the development of new technologies; and to move the Chinese economy from its current resource- and energy-intensive condition toward being more sustainable and environmentally friendly. This doesn't mean BYD will necessarily benefit from direct government support (though it might), but it means that the interests of the company and the country will mesh.

Since it was founded, BYD has operated at the liberalized end of the product market freedom matrix, first in developing a core component of mobile handsets, and now with electric cars, neither of which has been subject to heavy-handed official regulation. Throughout its various incarnations—as a component manufacturer, research-based company, and full-scale automobile company—it has built its business model around serving the huge emerging market of Chinese looking to buy their first car. BYD's product is also aligned with the needs of cities and their governments around the country that want to develop their own transport sectors but are increasingly concerned about the environmental and other costs posed by traditional cars.

No one, including Wang himself, is 100 percent sure about how sustainable BYD's growth will be. But whether or not Wang ultimately turns out to be right or wrong in his extraordinary vision, he is positioning BYD to thrive no matter how the auto industry evolves. If he succeeds, it will be because of the company's versatility. BYD may prosper as a battery component manufacturer, or a manufacturer of vehicles for China, or as a global electric carmaker. Because of its willingness to innovate in all these domains, the possibilities of accomplishing all three cannot be written off. And even at this early and uncertain stage, the BYD story illustrates an important quality of Chinese entrepreneurs: the versatility that carries them forward through a wide range of rapidly changing circumstances.

Versatility in business is the source of the ability to shift course with confidence. It reflects a broad set of skills and capabilities, and the judgment needed to apply them to a wide variety of problems and lines of business. In cultivating versatility, there are seven broad organizational attributes that company leaders can set out to develop:

1. Mental Fluidity and Resilience

This is the ability to juggle simultaneously the multiple practices required to move toward a long-term goal. For example, BYD has a clear capability in low-cost manufacturing, established through its battery business, which it is now applying to full-scale vehicle production. Many of these building blocks—distinctive marketing, manufacturing, innovation, or other capabilities—will have to be rethought and rebuilt as the company advances, and on occasion even the long-term goals will have to be rewritten. Leaders with mental resilience have the toughness necessary to cope with these changes and not abandon a company's vision when faced with day-to-day challenges or the pressure to settle for lesser objectives.

Such flexible, resilient leadership is at a premium anywhere in the world, but in most countries the knowns are largely fixed, and the unknowns are at least guessable; in China, the knowns themselves can change, and the unknowns can remain unknown. In early 2008, for example, after several years of rising costs for labor and materials (and exacerbated by the appreciation of the yuan against the dollar), many manufacturers started to think about relocating some of their manufacturing operations to other countries.

But the onset of the global economic crisis changed their minds. By mid-2009, as exports from China fell sharply, sourcing-centric companies found themselves looking at China's own consumer markets, where although demand had also weakened, the decline was nothing like that which had taken place in Europe and America.

Here was a major new opportunity—or was it? New uncertainties emerged. How fast could China shift to becoming a more consumption-driven economy? How effectively would the government's massive stimulus package be spent, especially given its weighting toward infrastructure and the potential for corruption and other bureaucratic inefficiencies? How would China's stance on foreign ownership of companies within its borders evolve, especially given similar tensions in the United States and Europe?

In the financial sector, would the government continue deregulation, or retrench? How would the government respond to concerns that stakes in many strategic state-owned enterprises were being sold too cheaply or easily to overseas businesses? Would these sales continue, or would they be slowed down or even stopped?

In other sectors, would a greater tendency to protect Chinese industries emerge? The government had refused to allow the Carlyle Group's bid for the Xugong Group, one of the country's largest makers of heavy machinery, or Coca-Cola's bid for Huiyuan Juice to go forward. Would it continue to ban similar deals?

These uncertainties left many multinational companies with a dilemma: choosing whether to raise their commitments in China or retrench their portfolios. For some, headquarter-driven business reviews led to the pruning of investments deemed noncore, but others set about expanding their business in China as they cut back elsewhere. DHL, for example, owned by Germany's Deutsche Post, in late 2008 shut down its express delivery service within the United States. But it remained keen to expand in Asia, tapping growing intracountry demand, especially in China, which the company describes as an "an absolute must-have." To do this, it sought to acquire local rivals or form joint ventures.

Indeed, a number of companies kept expanding in China, including the Carlyle Group, which spent $20 million on a 10 percent stake in El-lassay, a high-end Chinese women's fashion house, in early 2009. Royal DSM, a life and material sciences company from the Netherlands, bought 10 percent of North China Pharmaceutical Group in a deal worth $110 million; and Yum! Brands acquired 20 percent of Little Sheep, an Inner Mongolia–based hot-pot business with a few hundred outlets around China, for $634 million.[3] Coca-Cola, for its part, announced in March 2009 that it would invest $2 billion in China in the following three years. The scale of this investment plan surpassed the total value of investment the company had made in the previous thirty years, since returning to China in 1979. Earlier the same year, PepsiCo also announced a plan to invest $1 billion over four years to expand its capacity in the country's inland and far western provinces. Novo Nordisk announced it would spend $400 million on an insulin plant in Tianjin, which will be the company's main Asia-Pacific manufacturing hub. Bayer Schering Parma declared its commitment to invest $139 million over five years in a Beijing R&D center.

The list could go on, including many more examples of companies committing investment to China despite the world's economic slowdown. It is worth noting, however, that the latest round of deals have a different nature than those conducted just two years before. Many involve previously untapped geographies. The government's emphasis on boosting their development as part of its stimulus program has led to the creation of some substantial new markets. There has also been a shift in focus to raising consumer spending, with subsidies given to a wide range of electronic and white goods. Financial services have also benefited. Previously, banks largely concentrated on urban areas in eastern coastal provinces. As a result credit availability for rural small- and medium-sized enterprises (SMEs) was highly restricted. Most of the financial services available in rural areas came from rural credit cooperatives, the Postal Savings Bank, and the Agricultural Bank of China, all of which are among the least innovative of state-owned banks. HSBC, however, has opened three rural banks and received approval for a fourth, seeking to bring its international experience to countryside markets and support the development of a sustainable rural economy.

Other possibilities come from Chinese companies now looking to invest in business around the world, especially in Asia and other emerging markets. Although they know the economic crisis has created many excellent buying opportunities, the leaders of these businesses are aware of the challenges they face to make acquisitions work. This creates opportunities for international firms to help them with everything from partner search and due diligence to postmerger integration.

Global companies with the right range of abilities and capabilities—those that can devote time and resources to China despite the demands being placed on them elsewhere, that have a product or service that attracts Chinese consumers, or that have something to offer Chinese corporate partners—could find themselves in a strong position to reap the benefits of their prior investments there. But they would almost certainly have to rework their previous plans—swapping an emphasis on markets in one set of regions for another, say, or looking to change large parts of their product range. In such circumstances, companies need to demonstrate fluidity of mind: the ability to change and amend their thinking and projects on the fly.

A fluid mind is not reactive, in the sense of thoughtlessly bending to events in panic or greed, but is capable of changing easily and tends to change when needed. The reactive response to rapidly changing circumstances was summed up for me by the former China head of an American consumer goods company: "For most companies, this instability and dynamism will call for trial-and-error responses to problems. A lot of time will inevitably be spent firefighting: managing on the run in order to keep up with the exigencies of the business." And undoubtedly, many corporate leaders and managers will take this approach.

But "firefighting" is not fluidity of mind. Executives who try to stay on top of changes at the ground level, tackling one opportunity or problem at a time, will find themselves sucked into the minutiae of their businesses and will lose sight of their overall strategy and context.

Another approach is to focus on one core task, ignoring other opportunities. But the Chinese environment may not permit this. The country and its markets are so diverse that most companies will need to work on multiple fronts simultaneously.

There is another way, one adopted by many Chinese companies, that emphasizes standing back and look for ways of viewing relevant trends and events in a holistic fashion. Exactly how to apply such a technique will have to be figured out by every individual company depending on its own circumstances and needs. But the general methodology should stand most companies in good stead. Step back and map out the array of forces at play and the relations among them: the major trends shaping the country, as described in chapters 2–5 of this book, and their particular relationship to your own industry and markets. Then use this map to make sense of the complex array of changing situations that you face. Consider in particular the possible influences at play and how likely—or unlikely—changes could impact your business.

This has little to do with making predictions, most of which, as was noted in the last chapter, are likely to be proved wrong. Rather, it is about looking at the kind of scenarios that might arise and then how best to prepare for meeting their multiple possibilities. Keep your overall goals and objectives clear and constant; like BYD, hold an aspiration that can easily be stated and defended, and that doesn't easily change. But allow your strategies to be flexible: reacting to changing circumstances, accommodating new information and data as they become available, and remaining aware of the impact of shifts in the supply chain, the markets, the government, or the world at large.

2. Speed of Action and Organizational Nimbleness

Mental fluidity is not enough by itself. Companies need to be able to act and react quickly and nimbly when things turn out differently from what was expected. This is particularly important in China, where business takes place on a greater scale than almost anywhere else in the world. When an opportunity arises, it can be of a magnitude that will test the abilities of most businesses to cope.

For example, when the number of mobile-phone users surged in the early 2000s, the market share of foreign companies dropped from 95 percent to less than half. Nokia, Motorola, Ericsson, Alcatel, and Siemens simply weren't prepared for the growth in demand that came as the operators rolled out networks and slashed tariffs. Into their place stepped Chinese companies able to make low-cost phones using off-the-shelf components. A large part of Nokia's current dominance of the Chinese market can be traced to its reaction to those events. It centralized production at one location in Beijing, invested heavily in development capacity there so that now it can produce several new phones each month, added a wide range of low-cost models, and reworked its retail model, building out links to a network of outlets across the entire country.

Other bursts of market dynamism continue to occur. Over the next decade, industry after industry, and not just those that have been opened to competition, face futures of multiple shakeouts through mergers, acquisitions, consolidations, and closures. Markets will continue to grow as more people move into cities and into the income bracket that allows them to become consumers.

The tire industry provides a good example of how companies missed a huge opportunity because of their inability to react quickly enough. Earlier this decade, most industry experts believed automobile purchases would grow at around 15–20 percent annually. But this figure was just an educated guess. Much to everyone's surprise, up until the global economic crisis, annual growth was around twice this on average, and as high as 75 percent in one year. None of the world's leading tire-making companies present in China were prepared for this. Suddenly they were all caught by surprise, missing a huge opportunity for growth and market share gains. They responded by overcompensating, creating massive new facilities. Toward the end of 2008, however, sales growth plunged, leaving many of these companies facing significant short-term overcapacity and perhaps long-term structural overcapacity should demand growth continue to be slow. Then, in 2009, the auto market started to surge again, turning China, as we've seen, into the world's largest vehicle market.[4] Auto makers and suppliers, including tire manufacturers, have rushed to meet this surging demand. Finally, there is still a risk, however, that their new production lines could lead to overcapacity. Exacerbating the risk is the fact that much of this jump in demand can be attributed to government stimulus measures, which in turn have led some industry observers to ask how sustainable the increase in market size is likely to be.

Boom. Bust. Rise. Fall. The kind of fluidity that can respond to a massive upshift (to 75 percent growth) and then a rapid downshift is tough to achieve. But there are a growing number of success stories from companies that have managed to accomplish this. KFC was careful to get its business formula right before rolling out across China with major investments. Starbucks built fluidity into its entry-and-growth model in China; it chose to conduct joint ventures in a couple of key entry cities as a way to hedge against potential losses, while buying an option on the upside through an agreement that allowed it to buy out its partners. GM's success in China can be attributed in large part to its noted fluid mindset in this country. Among Chinese auto companies, Chery and Geely have been noted for their fluidity—for example, in the ways they have revitalized their brands when facing low-cost competition.

Another reason for fluidity is the rapid changes that can occur at a very large scale, such as in consumer tastes, as people get used to goods and foods that they were unfamiliar with before. One example is milk. A decade ago, milk was sold in powder form; there was no suitable packaging to allow for long-distance transportation. As new processes such as UHT and pasteurization were introduced, the liquid milk market took off exponentially. Despite the 2008 scandal over the widespread lacing of milk with the industrial chemical melamine in order to falsify protein levels, milk is now a regular part of the diet for many Chinese, especially children. The country's best dairy companies, such as Mengniu and Yili, remain both profitable and fast growing. In 2008, for instance, Mengniu became the largest customer in the world for Tetra Pak, the liquid-packaging supplier.

Regulatory change will further shake up the way companies distribute and sell their goods. In some areas, older, local government-run systems still dominate distribution; in others newer private companies are filling gaps in the market. In city after city across the country, the socialist-era retail system based around small stores and state-run department stores is giving way to another one, with Chinese and foreign supermarket chains snaking out across the country, twenty-four-hour convenience stores springing up on every urban corner, and malls being built way in advance of demand in many districts.

Fragmentation is common in distribution systems. Few transport companies have anything more than a local reach. The only national ones are hugely inefficient state-owned giants. Companies that want to reach second-, third-, and fourth-tier cities must either manage a myriad of local distributors or build a distribution system themselves. There is no single answer to this. Coca-Cola set about moving its drinks to retailers by signing bottling agreements with different companies in different parts of the country. Procter & Gamble, the most successful fast-moving consumer goods company in China, does its distribution itself, as does KFC. But few companies have the same volume of goods to move as Procter & Gamble or 2,600-plus outlets to move them to, as KFC has. Even fewer would want to devote valuable management time to building up a series of skills in functions they typically outsource to third-party contractors in other markets. But China often calls for companies having to question the practices they hold dear in other parts of the world, and coming up with a different answer.

Putting an even greater premium on mental fluidity over the next decade will be the changes in Chinese society and official China's approach to governance. Urbanization and the embrace of sustainable growth (with far fewer carbon emissions) will lead to some major changes in the business environment. There will be a reworking of many of the regulatory frameworks in which companies operate, most likely including a tightening of environmental controls, a greater emphasis on social equity, and greater government involvement in certain industries and sectors, such as those to do with energy. Certainly, China will see far less of the freewheeling "anything goes" attitude of the last two decades, and the gradual adoption of economically and environmentally sustainable practices across an ever wider range of activities.

Economic liberalization itself may shift in unprecedented ways. In the 1990s, Zhu Rongji drove the country toward liberalization because of his belief in the hazards of trying to protect industries from competition, be it domestic or foreign. The restructuring of the state sector that followed proved him right, but the benefits Zhu was aiming for have by and large been realized. Now, as the government searches for a more sustainable growth model, it wants to be more selective about which sectors it opens and to what extent, particularly in key sectors such as banking. China will continue to open businesses, but it will do so more on its own terms, where it sees clear benefits for itself or its companies.

Official moves toward the establishment of a "harmonious society" will lead to companies having to change their practices, from growth at all costs to also balancing their own needs with those of society. As development priorities change, officials are likely to look for ways in which they can exert greater influence. This won't lead to a return to central planning, but it will lead to stricter forms of regulation or other changes. The government's growing interest in restricting transfer pricing has already been noted; individual taxation is another area of change. Since 2007, everyone with an income of Rmb120,000 (around $17,600) or more has had to file an annual tax return.[5]

Business competition can lead to equally sharp surprises. Many multinational corporations have entered China unprepared for the fierce competitors they find there, and all too capable of underestimating them. Whirlpool lost against Haier and other Chinese competitors; eBay was deflected by Taobao; and even Coca-Cola and Pepsi have been challenged by such local companies as Wanglaoji and Kangshifu.

The most mentally fluid corporate leaders will keep multiple scenarios in mind, ready to react rapidly as they come to fruition. Sometimes entering a market via an acquisition will be the way to respond to a new opportunity; sometimes building through organic growth will be the right answer; sometimes the best option will be teaming up with another company. Having the scenarios in place will encourage companies to build the necessary capabilities before they are needed.

ICI Paints, a part of Akzo Nobel, has high aspirations for the China market: it wants growth of three times the average market growth rate. To meet this target, it must enhance its core position in the country's more mature markets, and it must expand into less-developed regions where growth will be faster. This calls for entering new product categories tailored for the lower end of the market while continuing to build its premium products. As a result, it has found itself no longer managing a single paint business but instead running a portfolio of businesses at different stages of maturity. To handle this situation, the company has realigned its entire organization. Its more mature businesses have been granted greater independence, and a new corporate development group was set up to oversee the higher-growth regions, lending support for everything from business-model development and strategic planning to project management. Substantial senior management time and resources are being invested to grow these emerging businesses and develop the specific capabilities they need. Once a business reaches maturity, it will be spun off and integrated alongside the company's other mature businesses.

Fluidity can also be highly practical. For example, rapidly improving the functioning of a supply chain—for example, with better logistics or network design—can bring sizable returns, especially if this allows companies overnight expansion or change of what they make. Many companies recognize the opportunities inherent in having a dual-mode sales-sourcing business in China, fully integrated into their global operations, but they have yet to develop the lean, flexible, integrated supply chains necessary to deliver on that potential. A study conducted by Booz & Company found that only one in six multinational manufacturers operating in China had applied postponement and segmentation methodologies to their logistics systems; most companies can realize major gains in efficiency. Building more flexibility into operations can also help overcome the problems faced by all companies in China, such as staff issues, product safety and quality, counterfeiting, and intellectual property theft.

The fluidity needed to meet the Chinese business environment can sometimes contradict well-established, ingrained, and previously successful ways of thinking. Chen Hong, the CEO of SAIC Motor, once remarked that while Japanese and Korean automotive makers took twenty to thirty years to develop their products, technologies, and quality standards, building scale and incorporating the skills necessary for their industry gradually, Chinese auto makers such as SAIC need to tackle all these challenges at the same time. In a similar vein, the strategy director of a major foreign automotive maker has commented that although his company is currently selling around one million cars a year annually in China, he expected this number to double within a few years; to support this extra volume would require his company to establish an entirely new operational structure.

The practices of the best Chinese companies offer some lessons in how to combine mental fluidity and operational flexibility. Haier's move into international markets was made by using the same advantages it had used to grow domestically—niche products produced in volume and then sold at a low price—but recast for the differing needs of its new target consumers. In one celebrated example, it captured two-thirds of the American wine refrigerator market by targeting a business that most appliance companies had seen as too niche-scale to bother with. By lowering prices to a fraction of competitors' prices, it created a volume business.

3. Coordination of Operations Among Markets

Geographical opportunities can vary dramatically in China, and they can also change rapidly. For some companies, one year Shanghai will be hot, the next it will be Chengdu. As we saw in chapter 2, companies that have focused principally on the three current centers of wealth—the Bohai rim region centered on Beijing and Tianjin in the north, the Yangtze Delta in the east, and the Pearl River Delta in the south—will have to extend their reach inland. This will mean managing and coordinating operations at very different stages of development, in different circumstances, and in different parts of the country—but all at the same time.

Many businesspeople are already aware of the differences among Chinese regions; for example, the far west, the coastal east, the subtropical south, and the dry north. But there is also tremendous diversity within regions. Even in the wealthiest of coastal provinces, larger cities are very different from smaller towns. A half-hour drive outside a large city can take you to a far more modest local economy and less sophisticated commercial environment. China's breathtaking economic growth, which has transformed the major cities at a breakneck pace, has exacerbated many of these differences and made it harder to plan for growth.

Many companies will move into lower- and midtier markets earlier than they would in other countries. There are two reason for this: first, because of their scale and growth potential, and second, because of the threat posed by domestic companies establishing themselves in these markets and then using them as their foundations for moving up into higher-tier markets. This can be a successful strategy, but so can the move from high- to low-tier markets, depending on the industry and competitive dynamics.

ICI Paints built a strong position in high-end emulsion products in the early 2000s, investing heavily in tier-one cities. By 2005, more than 40 percent of its China sales came from these well-developed cities. Then, to maintain its high growth rate, ICI started selling lower-end products to lower-tier cities, reaching its customers through traditional outlets such as Mom-and-Pop shops. Its goal for 2010 is to have tier-three cities accounting for 30 percent of sales, with tier-one cities accounting for just around 20 percent.

Nippon Paint, in contrast, invested heavily in lower-tier markets early on, to the extent that more than 30 percent of its sales were coming from tier-three cities by 2005. Since then, it has been looking to increase its share in the higher-end market. In 2006, it invested heavily in the launch of its odorless products aimed at wealthier consumers in tier-one regions. Despite their different approaches, both ICI Paints and Nippon Paint have emerged as the top players in the China paint market, with neither yet to emerge as the clear leader.

Developing goods for this wide range of markets is often best accomplished by establishing in-country research and development teams. These, however, will have to be given mandates different from those of their home-country R&D staff. Most research in developed countries is focused on producing new or high-end goods; in China, the emphasis is more on producing goods for other tiers, ones that its consumers can afford.

In some ways, thinking of China's regions as separate countries helps; they are each as large as many other countries. But this view is also partly misleading; markets overlap among many of them, as can distribution networks. And underneath it all they are part of a single nation, with one currency and one government. The longer-term trend will be for greater unity as communications and transport networks develop.

Distinguishing the factors that link and separate adjoining regions is already an important part of any marketing strategy. Toyota has realized this: its two major carmaking plants in China lie around 1,200 miles apart; one is in the northern city of Tianjin and the other in the southern city of Guangzhou. When it set up in Guangzhou, it arranged for a special port to be built to move cars between the two locations and make it easier to serve each end of the country.

4. Constant Monitoring of New Developments

Some companies in China have built success on S curves. Through foresight and good fortune, they were present at the start of a surge of hypergrowth in their product lines, then rode an immense wave of demand to market dominance. Examples already discussed in this book include mobile communications, mortgages, and passenger cars. The Chinese economy is so complex that reliably forecasting such S curves is all but impossible. Nonetheless, this does not mean that a company cannot put itself in a better position to anticipate the possibilities of such sudden surges occurring. Spotting and managing discontinuities within market segments through the triangulation of available data is paramount, while regulatory changes affecting an industry have proved to be one of the main triggers of growth, underlining how important it is for companies to monitor what is happening at a policy level in their industry.

Similarly, understanding social and cultural shifts is important because it can help you identify when attitudes are shifting dramatically toward a particular product. (Consider the rapid cultural changes that had to occur for milk to suddenly be popular.) Metrics and context form the core of market knowledge, and a company's ongoing ability to capture market knowledge, and act on it, will be one of the keys to success. Developing and institutionalizing this capability requires a systematic yet entrepreneurial approach, usually calling for the building of a market research team on the ground.

Even companies with well-established practices still need to adjust their research methodologies frequently. There are several reasons for this: demand is often latent, the supply side remains highly unpredictable, and proper metrics and market segmentation often remain undefined. Given all this, companies often need to make a trade-off between making a prompt decision and collecting enough data to confirm or negate hunches. The most effective companies have executives who spend much of their time on the ground—going to trade shows, talking to customers, visiting different markets, and finding out what their competitors are doing.

Unfortunately, many foreign executives, instead of spending time out scouting the marketplace, spend far too many hours in their offices, demanding that reams of data be delivered to their desks so that they can make decisions, but ignorant of just how much of this data is incomplete or outdated by the time it is presented to them. By eschewing in-person fieldwork, these executives generally lack the judgment to make the right decisions when the market information is incomplete or ambiguous. Doug Jackson, head of China for Coca-Cola, is an excellent example of someone who has their nose on the ground. Since his arrival in China, he has traveled extensively across the country visiting both larger and smaller cities with the aim of trying to understand the market, his customers, and the channels to market.

Even the shortest of journeys can generate valuable and surprising insights that published data cannot provide. The China head of one of the world's largest consumer goods companies talks of the disparity he found on driving half an hour from the center of a major city where his company had just opened a key production center. Despite his company having had a China presence for more than two decades, including spending tens of millions of dollars on advertising, he found that retailers on the outskirts of this city had negligible awareness of his company's brands.

Because it is so important to capture evolving market information, the best companies in China make a point of encouraging formal and informal exchanges of market and regulatory information within their organizations, often among people in the field and across different organizational units, so the most can be made of what information they do gather. They know that building up market knowledge over time eventually puts a company in a position to make a big bet.

5. Managing Human Capital

While many companies are quick to praise the talent and industriousness of their staff in public, in private executives often admit to a list of grievances about human capital. Managing people is and will continue to be one of the hardest challenges confronting most companies in China.

The most immediate issue is the short supply of skilled and experienced staff, especially managers and professionals, a problem that will be further exacerbated as the economy continues to grow. While companies such as IBM have tapped into China's growing number of educated, skilled engineers and technical people for its R&D and procurement teams, the competition for these individuals is intense and will become more so.

But in the longer term, an even harder challenge will be that of reworking attitudes. Chinese society has been through many wrenching changes during the last several decades. This is continuing as urbanization of a previously rural population. The instability and change that creates opportunities also leads individuals to question their loyalty to the institutions around them. As many people have pointed out, this has left many individuals in a spiritual vacuum, uncertain of both their personal aspirations and of the social mores around them.

Particularly problematic are the outlooks of many people in their twenties, thirties, and forties. A combination of the destruction of much of China's social fabric during the cultural revolution of the 1960s and early 1970s and the "get rich fast" mentality of the 1980s and 1990s has produced a generation with little respect for traditional community-oriented values. Its cynicism is manifest in everything from job hopping and misplaced salary expectations to staff who, when offered an evening meal allowance if they work past 8:00 p.m., systematically clock off at 8.01 p.m.

Multinational companies must be aware of the larger context and be creative in thinking of ways of solving these problems. Under China's current conditions, building teams and team spirit is unlikely to be straightforward. A lot of time and effort will be necessary, often spent one-on-one with talented staff.

Employee rights have also been enhanced with a new labor law that came into effect in 2008. Dismissing staff is far harder than it was previously, as is hiring people on a temporary basis. While there have been widespread complaints that the law pushes up staff costs, it should also contribute to creating more stable workforces, and ultimately act as a stimulus encouraging companies to move up the value chain. This gives companies more reason to focus more attention on hiring the right people and to invest in corporate learning and other ways to improve the quality of their staff.

Multinationals may benefit from understanding the mores of Chinese businesses. From the outside, many domestic companies appear to be operating in a transitional manner: modernizing, but still subject to many traditional constraints. Consider the differences between the prevailing culture in Chinese companies and that of businesses in developed economies (see exhibit 7-1).

These cultural differences help explain why some mergers and acquisitions go well and others go poorly. Deliberate attention to bridging the divide can make all the difference in postmerger integration or the management of joint ventures. In the short term, companies may benefit from adopting a more Chinese approach. Most Chinese employees are used to being told what to do. Asking them to be creative and come up with their own answers to problems may result in bemusement and confusion. However, companies should be wary of adopting such practices as a long-term model. In the long run, China will move away from its traditional corporate structures; to move up the value chain, companies will have to develop a broader range of innovation and creativity, which will require empowering staff.

These changes will take time. While many multinationals talk about their commitment to China as being for the long term, when it comes to human resources, it absolutely has to be. As a consequence, multinational companies must make training a huge part of their China commitment, even if they find that the price of producing the next generation of Chinese managers and executives is that many of these

EXHIBIT 7-1 The gap in business culture

Chinese Business Culture	Multinational Business Culture
Fast decision making in response to dynamic market	Greater emphasis on planning and analysis
Large use of rules of thumb such as "80/20"	More precision in planning and decision making
Widespread use of imitation, sometimes as a starting point for innovation	Compliance with intellectual property; innovation centric
Top-down hierarchies, with an emphasis on direction	Flatter reporting, with an emphasis on teamwork
Leader is often "supreme leader"	Leader is often a coach
"Rule by man," with decisions often taken arbitrarily	Clearer systems and policies
Values based on traditional hierarchical relationships; individual rights secondary to those of the organization	Values based on integrity, trust, value to clients, and return to shareholders

Source: Booz & Company

people leave to work for other companies or establish their own competing businesses.

Many companies have already taken such a position. Motorola did so as far back as 1993, when it set up Motorola University China; others have followed. Delivery company TNT has its TNT China University; Microsoft has spent tens of millions of dollars offering training to tens of thousands of Chinese software engineers; and the Nokia Research Center has set up its first long-term research facility in Asia at Beijing's Tsinghua University, bringing together some twenty of its researchers with thirty of the university's professors and fifty of its students.[6]

6. Establishing and Maintaining Relationships in China

In America and Europe, contracts form the heart of any business arrangement; in China, relationships are still the most important factor. True, *guanxi* (personal connections) don't have the same importance as they did twenty years ago, when getting almost anything done seemed to need a "fixer" of one kind or another. But because of the way Chinese business culture operates, turning on the intricate play of the ties among a host of people and organizations, the cultivation of connections and relationships will remain an important factor for decades to come.

Superficially, this isn't so different from elsewhere. Worldwide, large companies in sensitive industries have to pay attention to keeping on good terms with officials. But in China, both the reasons for developing relationships with officials and the ways in which they are managed are very different. The most important thing to bear in mind when handling official relations stems from the relationship between the business community and the government. Official China, for both traditional cultural reasons and ideological ones, sees itself as standing at the core of all important decisions to do with the running of the country in general and the economy in particular. Government officials, central and local, therefore *have* to be involved; they cannot be ignored or circumvented. Even in the most liberalized of industries, they see themselves as having a duty to oversee and, where necessary, shape events, as seen in the Ministry of Commerce's decision to veto Coca-Cola's takeover of Huiyuan Juice.

In regulated sectors in particular, establishing long-term relationships with official China is important. Even more important is staying attuned to the changing structures of the industry, which determine how the relationships evolve. In energy and finance, for example, official involvement is overt, and will remain so. The global financial crisis has reinforced beliefs that companies, especially banks, should not be left to their own devices, but must be monitored. Companies that had therefore assumed that their sector was likely to become more liberalized must take another look at their plans and see if they need rethinking. Consequently, for many companies, finding the right corporate partner (or partners) is likely to become more important, not less so. Establishing relationships involves finding partners who share a company's vision. Doing this can take several years, but spending time like this is the only way a company can be confident it is on the right path for a long-term commitment to China.

Whenever a company looks at a project, it has to consider the benefits the project will have for various partners and stakeholders. Given the length of time it takes for many projects to reach the point where returns are satisfactory, long-term win-win deals are the only kind that will ultimately work. This is particularly the case in China's most tightly regulated sectors, but lining up support from officials is also critical in more liberalized industries. Most of this lobbying has to be done behind the scenes, getting to know possible partners and projects, and the officials involved. This can pay off in multiple ways, among them being able to spot potential changes in rules or regulations earlier than other companies. As noted in chapter 4, the goal of official China isn't a laissez-faire economy per se, but a successful, powerful, and modern economy. Companies can develop relationships with officials and Chinese companies by projecting and substantiating the message that their success in China is good for the country as a whole. Those that do this will always do better than those that focus solely on their own bottom lines.

And as noted before, a heavily regulated economy does not necessarily mean it is static. Changes in regulated sectors can happen fast and be even more sweeping than in liberalized industries. In the oil and petrochemicals sector, for instance, until just over a decade ago the industry was divided between CNPC, the country's principal oil and gas producer, which operated upstream, finding and developing oil and gas fields, and Sinopec, which operated downstream, running refining and petrochemical facilities. A third company, CNOOC was responsible, as its name suggested, for offshore oil and gas production. The government ended this demarcation, reshuffling assets among Sinopec and CNPC, allowing all three to operate up- and downstream and subsequently allowing them each to list subsidiaries on international stock markets. The industry became highly competitive as a result. All three companies, plus ChemChina (formerly the country's main chemicals trader), started to establish refineries and other petrochemical operations.

This placed foreign energy companies in a difficult position. It was no longer clear what they would be able to do, when they might be able to do it, and how they should position themselves. In such circumstances, a multinational company is unlikely to pull off a business coup singlehanded: if it enjoys success, then it will likely have to share it with a Chinese partner.

7. Running Janus-Faced Operations

Janus, the Roman god able to see in two directions simultaneously because of his pair of faces on the front and back of his head, epitomizes what the most successful global companies doing business in China have in common: an ability to run integrated operations that simultaneously look in toward China and its possibilities and outward elsewhere to see how these China strengths can be leveraged globally.

Honeywell has this outlook; it creates products within China that can be sold to the rest of the world. IBM has it, but for functions rather than products. Nokia also has been successful by deploying China's production advantages to make low-cost phones for the China market, then using this as a foundation for transforming itself into a company that can sell at every value point on the mobile handset product range worldwide, not just at the top tier where it had previously existed.

A handful of Chinese companies are taking similar approaches. BYD, Huawei, and ZTE, for example, have used their expertise at building businesses within China to establish themselves elsewhere. Huawei and ZTE became major forces in the telecommunications industries of developing markets around the world and from this foundation began to enter developed-country markets. Lenovo, through its acquisition of IBM's personal computer business, is trying to do the same.

This twin-faced approach requires a sense of purpose that extends beyond the bottom line. A short-term focus on profits can help a company achieve impressive results at first. But China's possibilities for transforming a company can only truly be appreciated by looking beyond this narrow perspective.

Many companies have failed to develop a longer-term outlook for operational reasons: unless things are kept as simple as possible, doing business in China is extremely hard. Such difficulties have to be surmounted; hence the importance of the other attributes in this chapter, notably the possession of fluidity and a holistic perspective.

As I noted in chapter 6, one factor that needs careful management is the relationship between China operations and headquarters. Many headquarters have little appreciation of the difficulties of just how to go about comprehending the opportunities China offers, and how large the scope is for misjudging what can happen, both on the upside and the downside. This state of affairs has little to do with the availability of information or data, and far more to do with being able to explain what is happening in the country in ways that both make sense and are actionable.

The rate of change in China often exacerbates miscommunications. The story of "China" that was told to headquarters last year may be very different from the "China" of this year, with a likelihood that it will have become yet another "China" in another twelve months. Expectations of what is possible will thus remain as much in flux as the country itself. Given the difficulties of having to explain exactly what is happening, the temptation for many China executives is "to go it alone": press on with their own plans, hoping things will work out and they will be able to surprise their boss with a major success. This isn't wise. It isolates China as a freestanding operation, keeps companies from working toward the global integration of their China operations, and can make it difficult for headquarters to provide up-to-date guidance and support when it really is necessary. Consequently, it is vital for companies to maintain proper communications and linkages with global headquarters. In this way, they can ensure corporate support at critical moments, smooth out daily operations, and manage longer-term expectations.

It will also be increasingly important to design decision rights so that Chinese operations can be fluid but globally integrated. For example, in most (but not necessarily all) cases, the China business unit leaders, rather than global leaders, should have primary authority over functions and product lines in China. This ensures faster decision-making and more successful execution. HQ should deploy capable executives to China, give them sufficient authority and resources, and keep the communications strong with the rest of the global enterprise.

The Effective Executive in China

Some extremely interesting research has been recently conducted by Nandani Lynton, a professor at Shanghai's China Europe International Business School, and Kirsten Høgh Thøgersen, a professor at Sun Yat-sen University in Guangzhou. They sought to identify the behavior and attitudes shared among the most effective international executives in China.[7]

They found a series of related attributes. Some three-quarters spoke Chinese, and 80 percent were fluent in three or more languages. Not just curious, these people were explicit about the importance of activities that give their minds free range, including reflection, reading nonbusiness materials, and focusing on music; and they welcomed new experiences.

Most of them sought opportunities to go overseas or grew up assuming they would move among countries. But they were also emotionally stable, with strong family and community ties (90 percent had marriages that had already lasted more than a decade; all contributed time or know-how to social or charitable organizations beyond their job). And every one of them shared resilient and positive outlooks on life.

The research also revealed five traits for successful executive behavior, and they will all probably resonate with readers of this book.

The first is possession of a holistic view of China that sees the country in terms of patterns formed among people and events rather than determined by causes and in need of explanations. The emphasis on being dispassionate such an approach fosters makes it easier to attribute successes to good fortune and failure to things being not quite as they had appeared when a decision was taken, which in turn helps companies respond flexibly rather than absolutely to events.

Second is an ability to switch rapidly between analytic and holistic thinking. Chinese business thinking doesn't call for throwing logic out of the window, but being able to sense when it's better to switch from a hard analytic mode to a softer holistic one.

Third, when actions are taken, decisiveness is important. Once you recognize an opportunity, respond with single-minded zeal. By multinational standards, Chinese companies often act on insufficient data; they rely instead on their finely tuned holistic picture and they trust in both their own and their group intuition. With this, they can then act wholeheartedly without having to endlessly evaluate and reevaluate. As Lynton and Thøgersen put it: "They are free to act quickly, to 'go.'" Of course, mistakes will be made, and in such circumstances it is also important to avoid attributing blame to individuals, or even the "community"; instead treat it as part of the learning experience that enriches the company as a whole.

Fourth is paying attention to people and their needs. Demonstrations of loyalty to staff are important, even if their loyalty to the company is uncertain. In general, treat business as a personal matter that is facilitated by showing respect. Particularly in Chinese companies, a high value is put on seeing everyone as permanent members of a community rather than as employees whose task is simply to fulfill their job descriptions.

Finally, it is important to have a perception of the bigger picture—beyond the individual and beyond your company—and with it the notion that something larger is occurring: the reestablishment of China in the world. We will return to this notion in more detail in the next chapter, but for now bear in mind that whereas in the West, particularly in the United States, a deep-rooted belief exists that progress stems from allowing competition among individuals, in China the notion is almost the opposite: that by working together, the best ideas can be strengthened, gaining the support they need along the way.

Lynton and Thøgersen conclude by suggesting that the mindset shared by successful executives in China may be the harbinger of a global mindset that corporate leaders need "to be successful in the integrated and competitive world of global business." I would go further than this. To be competitive, multinationals must learn from the ways in which Chinese companies cope with the unknowns and complexities of their business environment. It is the possibility of being able to see the holistic links between a company's business within China and its operations worldwide, and having the skills to make these links concrete, that will characterize one world management teams. These teams will be able to mix intuition and understanding, handle the risks, and act decisively and quickly in order to cope with the opportunities China will generate in the next decade. Finding the executives with such abilities will arguably be the single hardest task for any company. But the success of those companies that have managed this—as has been the case with KFC and Sam Su, Tetra Pak and Hudson Lee, Honeywell and Shane Tedjarati, and BYD and its visionary owner, Wang Chuanfu—shows what can be achieved.

CHAPTER 8

Vigilance

T HE STORY OF GOME, China's largest retailer of home appliances
and consumer electronics, is a remarkable tale of rapid rise—and
then turbulence and uncertainty. The company's origins stem from
the late 1980s, when founder and CEO Huang Guangyu left his home-
town in south China's Guangdong province to become an itinerant
trader. After traveling the length of the country, he opened a market
stall in Beijing selling electronic goods. The stall soon became a shop.
Relying on factories in his home province to supply him with cut-price
products, he turned the shop into a chain.

By 2008, GOME's 1,300 stores covered every corner of the country.
As China's largest electronic goods retailer, it accounted for 12 percent
of all electrical appliances sold according to the company's own internal estimates.[1] A lot of its growth came from acquisitions, which included taking over its third- and fourth-largest competitors.

Since 2004, the company has had a listing on the Hong Kong stock
exchange. Among its investors are Warburg Pincus Asia with 9.71
percent, JP Morgan with 8.88 percent, and Morgan Stanley with 8.17
percent. But Huang, also known by the Cantonese version of his
name, Wong Kwong Yu, just forty years old, remains by far the biggest
single shareholder, controlling (with his wife) more than 30 percent
of the company. Estimates of his wealth fluctuate, but by 2008 it was

put at around $6.3 billion, enough to make him one of China's wealthiest people.

Then, toward the end of 2008, Huang's fortunes changed overnight. In November, he disappeared. Gradually news emerged that he had been detained by the police in Beijing, apparently for "economic crimes" concerning the manipulation of share prices of two companies with ties to GOME. But no one seemed to know for sure. GOME representatives said he could not be contacted. Trading in the company's shares was halted in Hong Kong. Huang was suspended from his company duties and his wife, Du Juan, resigned as a director. In January, he resigned as company chairman, though he remained the largest shareholder.

As of the time of this writing in mid-2009, Huang remained detained, but trading had resumed in GOME's shares. Despite the economic slowdown and its legal troubles, the company had remained profitable, earning around $47 million on revenues of $1.4 billion in the first quarter of 2009. And in late June, it was announced that the Asian arm of Bain Capital would invest $417 million in the company. Bain Capital will become GOME's second-largest shareholder, with a stake of between 9.8 percent and 23.5 percent, assuming the full conversion of the convertible bonds. Through this investment, Bain Capital will also gain the right to nominate three non-executive directors to the board.

Such an investment has to be a gamble. GOME's future is uncertain; that of its biggest shareholder even more so. For anyone involved with the company—running it, owning it, working for it, or investing in it—nothing can be taken for granted other than it will remain a business in flux. Will Huang remain a shareholder? Could the company be closed down? Could it be forcibly taken over? Or can it continue to operate in the absence of its CEO and founder?

The particulars of the GOME case are extreme but, as we've seen throughout this book, this degree of dramatic change and uncertainty can be found everywhere in China. Many decisions are gambles. This will remain true for the foreseeable future. Companies and industries will rise in just a handful of years; some will then disappear even faster. Confronted with a multitude of opportunities and threats, businesses will have to be permanently on the lookout for anything that could transform their prospects, for better or worse.

Perpetual vigilance does not mean reacting to everything that happens. It means establishing a framework in which to be able to judge the importance of new events, and so being able to respond appropriately. By developing a mindset that recognizes the force of change and the context it creates for success, companies can best prepare their strategies for the coming decade.

Harvard professor Joseph Nye describes the requisite capability this way: "The most important skill for leaders will be contextual intelligence: a broad political skill that allows them successfully to combine hard and soft power into smart power and to choose the right mix of an inspirational and transactional style according to the needs of followers in different micro contexts."[2]

Nowhere will such a skill be more in demand than doing business in and with China or, for Chinese companies, in and with the rest of the world. It will not be enough for companies to be good at whatever it is they do; they will have to understand how their businesses fit into China's wider context.

In the rest of this chapter, I will draw a tentative picture of the future and where China is heading over the next decade, and possibly beyond. This is not a forecast—as I have noted before, all forecasts are likely to be proved wrong by events. Rather it is an identification of the key trends that all businesses will have to negotiate: the forces that will inevitably shape the environment.

Stable Momentum

As China negotiates its way through the fallout of the world's economic crisis, it is tempting to say that it faces a critical period: that the country stands at a crossroads, or some such phrase. Actually, this is anything but the case. China stood at a crossroads in the early 1990s. Then it was unclear, even to China's leaders, which direction the country should be taking. The decisions to embrace economic reform wholeheartedly, restructure China's industrial base and banking system, and join the World Trade Organization were momentous ones, and they took it down a path that the country has stayed on ever since.

Today, China's development, driven by its choices and by the resulting economic growth, has a momentum that it would be hard for anyone to stop, including the Chinese themselves. The country's broad trajectory for the next decade and beyond is readily discernible. Certainly its leaders will have to make major decisions that are difficult to face and resolve: how to secure energy supplies, reduce environmental depredation, make growth more sustainable, develop more responsive and transparent governance, deal with ethnic conflicts, build a more efficient and resilient financial system, and reduce the problems associated with corruption at all levels of officialdom. But these challenges all concern ways to improve the existing system, not pressure to change it for a new one.

The conclusion this points to, which must be stressed considering the number of pundits and experts predicting China's imminent collapse, is that the country does not face any systemic threats undermining the foundations of society. Clearly, there will be pressure for official China to make improvements in policy and management; in short, better governance, not different governance. The government already has far better machinery in place to handle its problems than it did a decade ago, thanks to the overhaul of the Communist Party's organization and membership described in chapter 4. As its efforts to manage environmental pollution and build a renewable energy industry show, it is already handling problems that seemed impossible to manage just a few years ago.

In general, China is now more stable socially and politically than it was in the late 1980s. As mentioned in chapter 4, a 2008 Pew Research

Center survey found that more than 80 percent of the Chinese population was satisfied with the country's direction and the general economy. This represented a rise from less than 50 percent satisfaction in a similar poll in 2002, and it far outpaces general satisfaction levels found in any other country.[3] True, some parts of Chinese society have prospered more than others, and unrest in Xinjiang and Tibet points to shortcomings in the country's treatment of minorities, but the lifting of hundreds of millions of people out of absolute poverty was a direct result of the government's policies of the last four decades and is recognized as such. Moreover, most people in China believe they can look forward to further improvements in their standard of living in the coming years.

But if China's overall social and political reform can be safely assumed to continue, this does not mean that companies can be complacent. Its domestic development remains at an early stage, and its international capability at an even earlier one. At home, China is advancing rapidly on many fronts. Structural changes in the economy, the demographics of the population, and the forms of governance are all in progress. An urban middle class has established itself in the wealthiest cities and is growing. Rural development has begun, albeit at a slower pace than its urban equivalent. Change within China will continue at different rates and with different degrees of success for decades to come.

Overseas, however, China's involvement in global affairs remains nascent. But the extent of its involvement will expand exponentially and at an accelerating rate. Talk of China reaching superpower status is premature in 2010; but it could happen. Even if it doesn't, China will inevitably play a key role in resolving the major international challenges of the first half of the twenty-first century, above all climate change. To date, the world's developed countries have been slow to involve China in many global forums; this will change as they find that China has both the economic power and the political influence to sit with them as an equal. There will be a learning process on both sides: Chinese officials will discover how best to exercise the power they have and the leaders of other countries will find ways to accommodate Chinese wishes and needs. The path is unlikely to be smooth, but given what is at stake, it will be in everyone's interests to develop frameworks capable of negotiating agreements aimed at establishing a true community of nations.

The Aftermath of Economic Crisis

In early and mid-2009, most observers predicted that it would take China several years to recover from the drop in external demand caused by recessions in the United States and Europe. It was apparent then that the years are over in which exaggerated American consumer demand could provide the financial base for China's growth in export industries. But recovery in China was already under way in late 2009. Making up for the shortfall were several factors within China.

First, the large stimulus program launched by the government in late 2008 made a difference. This is not simply a consumer support package or a short-term initiative. It will continue for three years, and most of the spending is dedicated toward increasing economic efficiency over the medium term. Of the Rmb 4 trillion (nearly US$600 billion) package announced by the government, 1.5 trillion is being spent on transport and power infrastructure, another trillion on postearthquake reconstruction, 400 billion on public housing and social welfare, 370 billion each on rural development and R&D (technology advancement), 210 billion on sustainable development, and 150 billion on educational and cultural projects, including health care improvement. Many of these investments were chosen for their long-term effects on the quality of life, productivity, and economic momentum of the country.[4]

Second, other sources than government expenditure will keep growth coming. Thanks to the restructuring of the financial system, banks can now lend in ways they couldn't a decade ago, while many companies, particularly large state-owned ones, had put aside a great deal of cash during the 2000s.

Third, after the huge investment of the last several years, industrial consolidation will inevitably occur. Many small and inefficient manufacturers will be taken over or will close down. This process is already taking place in export-oriented regions, particularly Guangdong. Through early 2009, tens of thousands of factories closed across the Pearl River Delta, leading to widespread forecasts of mass unemployment and possible unrest among migrant workers. Most of the companies that are closing are smaller, inefficient businesses. Stronger, more capable companies are surviving. These businesses are already improving their efficiency; they will emerge from the slowdown with larger market shares, leaner and more productive operations, and better quality standards.

The government would like to see a similar process happen in almost every industry. It has placed a three-year moratorium on new projects in the iron and steel sector. Overcapacity persists in the cement sector, and even new industries such as wind power and polysilicon have many redundant projects In short, almost everywhere you look there are many small companies that badly need consolidation to start realizing economies of scale and to create businesses large enough to invest in R&D as well as production.

Fourth, fears of widespread protectionism on the part of China, and consequent drops in growth, are likely to prove ill-founded. A more likely scenario is differentiation: officials will scrutinize merger and acquisition deals closely in terms of what they perceive as China's best interests. They will encourage takeovers, alliances, and partnerships that lead to improvements in practices and new technologies. Government leaders will also find other ways to reward or help companies that help China overcome its challenges: operating with economic efficiency, meeting environmental needs, increasing productivity, lowering resource usage, and so on.

China's sense of protectionism could turn out to be strategically defensive. For example, while foreign mergers and acquisitions will be possible, they will not necessarily be easier than they have been to date. The collapse of Chinalco's offer to buy into Rio Tinto, CNOOC's failure to buy Unocal, and the opposition that led to the Bain-Huawei buyout of 3Com being abandoned have taught Chinese officials that other governments can find regulatory or legal reasons to block deals. They are now putting in place similar regulations or policies to this effect as well.

Finally, the financial sector is likely to remain stable in China, in part because it is so carefully monitored. Since the summer of 2008, Official China's belief in close oversight of the financial sector has been reinforced. They will continue to stand by their conviction that the state must maintain strong control over the economy's "strategic heights." After seeing Western governments scurry to bail out banks and give support to other sectors during the global financial crisis, many Chinese officials felt vindicated: in their refusal to accept liberalization as a universal panacea for economic problems, in their decision to retain control of key aspects of the economy via ownership of China's very biggest companies, and in their maintenance of a largely nonconvertible currency. They continue to recognize the great value of market mechanisms, but they do not see these mechanisms as an end in themselves. In their view, the financial markets need to be supplemented by appropriate regulation, including capital-adequacy ratios that genuinely reflect the risks banks are undertaking (undistorted by off-balance sheet vehicles). The prime function of banks, in the view of official China, is to promote economic growth by allocating capital appropriately rather than trying to promote their own profitability independent of the "real" economy.

Thus, while the global financial crisis has affected China, it is not changing it; certainly not in the way it is reworking the United States and Europe. China will emerge from the crisis with a stronger, more efficient and more resilient economy: one that will rely as much on domestic as on foreign demand and that will be poised not just for continued growth but for more sustainable growth. And not only will it be more competitive, but it will also have a substantially larger share of the total world economy.

Despite these prospects, growth will probably not permanently return to the 10-percent-plus average annual rates that the country experienced before 2008. In the short term, such a figure may be reached, but over the coming years a rate of one or two percentage points less is likely as the economy matures. There will be some pluses in this. Wage pressures at the lower end of the scale are likely to ease. (Demand for experienced managerial and professional staff will remain intense.) Growth should also be less resource intensive. A huge share of the country's industrial expansion since 2000 took place in heavy industry, with the demand for steel, aluminum, chemicals, and other raw materials to supply the country's construction, automotive, and other manufacturing sectors. Most of these industries are in need of consolidation, with most of the smaller, more inefficient plants set either to close down or be taken over. More attention will be paid to developing a "green" economy through an emphasis on environmentally friendly practices and energy saving. This in turn should relieve some of China's resource and power needs, ending, for example, the electricity shortages that have affected most of the country since the mid-2000s.

But while overall the economy is likely to be more stable due to its more moderate growth rate, competition will intensify. Companies will have to get more out of their workforces, putting a greater emphasis on the use of better management and best practices. They will also find themselves gradually subjected to stronger regulation, with stricter enforcement of regulations already on China's statute books, for environmental protection, labor rights, intellectual property, and taxation.

The realization of all this has sunk in at some global companies. Many corporate leaders would like to increase their investment in China, because of its market growth prospects relative to the rest of the world. A survey of more than one hundred leading manufacturers conducted in late 2008 by Booz & Company found that more than half the respondents intended to commit further investment to China in the coming two years.[5]

But this money won't simply be spent adding capacity: many of these business leaders said they would be concentrating on improving their operations by raising standards and quality.[6] For the short run, these companies have accepted that weaker demand in China has made it impossible to offset shortfalls in exports immediately, but more than three-quarters of them said they felt that investing in China-based production now would bring better access to local consumers in the future.

Factors and Trends

Beyond the economic crisis, a new set of pressures and opportunities will matter to companies doing business in China. They will fall into three broad categories: those arising from market forces, the government, and the demographic evolution of the Chinese population.

Pressures arising from market forces will include land and labor costs. These may not rise much in 2009 or early 2010, due to the impact of the global financial crisis. But they will rise before long, as both the global economy and China's export sector recover. In the longer term, the cost of capital for Chinese companies will also inevitably increase.

There will also be corporate reforms, induced in part by the Chinese government and in part by businesses themselves, that will boost consumption and business development. Regulations are being introduced in 2009 to allow the establishment of consumer finance companies, and the big banks are all establishing small- and medium-sized lending arms. By the end of 2009, the Shenzhen stock market should have launched a market aimed at smaller companies, the Growth Enterprise Board. And it appears only to be a matter of time before farmers are allowed to use their land as security for mortgages; if this change goes ahead on a large scale, it will create an enormous potential pool of capital for rural businesses.

Pressures that stem more directly from the government will include tighter enforcement of environmental and other laws; stronger staff rights, as seen in the labor contract law, and increased costs for inputs. In many key areas, such as environmental restrictions and intellectual property, China already has a substantial body of law and supporting regulations in place, often with regulatory regimes as strong as those of many developed countries. But many multinationals are often cynical about Chinese attitudes, due to the weak or selective enforcement of many of its laws, most notably those protecting intellectual property and restricting pollution. Some foreign companies have striven to introduce global best practices in their manufacturing operations, only to see their domestic Chinese rivals either ignoring laws and failing to be punished, or bribing officials to overlook breaches of the law. The 2008 financial crisis exacerbated the problem, with local governments in particular becoming even laxer in their oversight of companies rather than doing anything that might result in a loss of jobs.

Nonetheless, the government is very serious about improving legal compliance across the board. For example, spurred by the high number of deaths in the mining industry, it set about closing small mines where safety rules are often ignored and most accidents take place. It has recognized how instances of pollution have affected both the economy and popular sentiment. The State Environmental Protection Administration has estimated the total cost of environmental pollution at around 10 percent of GDP; in 2008, a chemical plant at Xiamen on the Fujian coast was relocated following widespread protests the previous year.

At some point, the government will get serious and crack down on the smaller companies that either ignore the rules or cannot afford to get the equipment they need to comply with environmental regulations. When will this happen? When China has the resources. This is less a question of money and more of having people with the requisite experience. It takes a long time to put in place the training and oversight needed to develop skilled environmental inspection teams and enable them to work.

Foreign companies in particular will have to be vigilant about changes. For both political and financial reasons they are likely to be among the first targets of inspections. Evidence for this comes from another area where China is stepping up enforcement: taxation. In chapter 4, I noted how tax officials are scrutinizing the transfer pricing practices of only one hundred companies a year. These are mainly large multinationals. While their executives may complain that it's unfair to pick on them first, from China's point of view they are good targets for a host of reasons. First, these are high-profile businesses; finding and punishing just one foreign corporate lawbreaker would encourage many others to comply. Second, the amount of tax revenue involved is large, especially if businesses are spiriting money out of the country via their internal pricing practices. Third, these companies are already deeply experienced in handling transfer pricing issues: officials can expect them to know what is going on and behave appropriately. Fourth, these companies are not going to go away, unlike small Hong Kong or Taiwanese controlled plants, which could shut up shop overnight and whose owners could vanish without a trace. And, finally, it is far less likely that such companies would try and evade payments by offering bribes.

Other pressures stem from demographic factors, including the huge number of people moving to urban centers. This will lead to great increases in consumption in the coming decade: urban residents, with work commitments that cut back their time at home, tend to buy many more household products, packaged foods, and local services. In addition, starting around 2015, China will face a very different demographic challenge: that of an aging society. The number of people over the working age will grow fast. The pool of young workers that has driven growth in the last twenty years will begin to shrink, putting pressure on wages, and the number of retired dependents will rise. Currently, every one hundred people of working age have to support around forty dependents, either children or retirees. By 2040, that figure will have risen to sixty. As this happens, growth will inevitably slow.

To overcome the problems this will create, the government will have to place an even greater emphasis on education than it has already. (This is one reason China has increased its spending on schools so much in the last decade.) Companies will have to emphasize education, too. Currently, there are still benefits to be gained from looking to hire large numbers of unskilled young staff, but that won't hold true for much longer. Companies will have to look at ways of retaining older staff, possibly beyond retirement age. The upside will be a workforce that, though shrinking, will grow in ability. Throw in China's cultural proclivity in favor of education, and the result will be a transformation of the country's human resources in less than a generation, from a nation of farmers to a nation of educated, urban knowledge workers.

Finally, there are emerging government-driven imperatives on energy efficiency and autonomous business development. These will provide opportunties for both local and foreign investors and businesses—to help create wind power and electric vehicle innovation, for example, as well as strategic technical alliances and upgraded industrial processes.

All of these factors will put pressure on companies to improve their efficiency. Companies that have grown by adding scale will need to pay far more attention to increasing their productivity. Doing this will represent a particular challenge for Chinese companies, but foreign companies will also have to manage it deliberately. They will bring their best global management practices into the country. They will boost their marketing efforts, as sales to the Chinese markets start to grow in importance compared with exports. And they will continue to need to look for executives who can combine deep China experience with broad knowledge of business and management.

China and the World

Handling what happens in China will only be half the story. In the late 1980s, Kenichi Ohmae and other business experts argued that Japan was different from the West, and therefore that Western companies wanting to do business there needed to adapt and develop new ways of working. This turned out to be correct. But it will not be the same with China.

Businesses cannot treat China like a Japan in the 1980s and 1990s, as a place very different from everywhere else, where everything had to be tailored to Japanese needs. The reason for this is that China is integrating with the rest of the world in a way that Japan never managed to do.

This integration will be reinforced by the deepest aspects of Chinese culture. To be sure, outside its borders many people still see China as a kind of opposite culture to the West. But much of this impression stems from the impression left by 170 years of isolationism during the nineteenth and twentieth centuries, and especially the years of the Great Leap Forward and the Cultural Revolution. But these periods were not typical of the country's history. In general, the Chinese culture should not be seen as only, or even primarily, inward looking; the nation's history involves many long episodes of close integration with the rest of the world.

Already, the new phase of integration is taking place much faster and deeper, and on a much broader scale, than most people understand and appreciate. Having made it through the nineteenth and twentieth centuries, the Chinese want to say to the rest of the world, "Look, we're back." Their goal isn't the recreation of the old empire, or any empire, but a country that is and is treated as the equal of any other on the planet, and that through its achievements has earned the respect it deserves. Notions such as *decoupling*, a word used during the early part of the 2008 global financial crisis to suggest that the Chinese economy would continue to grow strongly despite the downturn elsewhere, underestimated the degree of integration that already existed. China was already dependent on the global economy, and most Chinese people were glad of that. They don't want to be isolated from the world; they want the world to know and respect them. And while China (and India) will continue to grow at a much faster economic rate than the developed economies, this will undoubtedly serve to integrate them further into the global economy, not to separate them.

Multinational companies will find Chinese companies to be extremely fast learners. Those operating in liberalized industries face more intense competition in their home markets than most multinationals do. They will struggle with some challenges: a lack of sophistication in planning and a lack of precision in their operations. But they also have strengths that can be easily adapted from China's turbulent markets, especially the abilities to operate in environments that are less than transparent and to make fast decisions.

A particularly important factor driving Chinese companies overseas will be the need to access capabilities and market knowledge. For Japanese companies, operating at a time when the pace of globalization was a lot slower than it now is, it was possible to delay starting overseas operations until the requisite technology or expertise had been acquired at home, and then to grow at a slow pace when starting up in a new market. Chinese companies do not have this luxury; their home market is not protected as Japan's was, and almost all markets around the world are far more open to competition than they were three decades ago.

To compensate, many Chinese companies will seek to learn through mergers and acquisitions. This will be relatively easy for them in the wake of the global financial crisis, when the opportunities for acquisition are great. In 2009, Lou Jiwei, the chairman and CEO of China's sovereign wealth fund, China Investment Corporation, spoke at the Boao Forum, a gathering of political and business leaders aimed at being an Asian equivalent of the Davos summit held annually in Switzerland. He told how, whereas a year before, investment opportunities, particularly in Europe, had always had many strings attached, now his fund was seen as a "lovable force," and he was hearing little talk of investment restrictions.

Recent examples of acquisitions aimed at meeting very specific needs were carmaker Geely's $40 million purchase of Australian company Drivetrain Systems International to strengthen its gearbox expertise and Bank of China's acquisition of Singapore Aircraft Leasing for its specialized know-how, in an area that the bank had yet to tackle. With much of the automotive industry in Europe and America in deep trouble, Chinese companies look highly likely to make some strategic purchases. Probably the most interesting possibility, at the time of this writing, is the potential purchase of GM's Hummer business by a privately owned machinery maker, Tenzhong, in the Sichuan province. Just as many foreign companies first gained experience of China by teaming up with a Chinese business, so Chinese companies are finding that buying a foreign company can both give them a foothold in a new market and an opportunity to discover different customer needs and ways of operating. When the goal is to build capabilities rather than scale, companies can focus on smaller deals, which are easier to handle and integrate with an existing business in China, a particularly important factor for companies with little knowledge of international business.

In the immediate future, most Chinese companies venturing overseas will concentrate on emerging markets. They may follow the models of deals such as that of China Mobile Pakistan, a wholly owned subsidiary of China Mobile, which teamed up with Alcatel-Lucent in early 2009 in a $53 million deal to provide mobile-phone services in northern Pakistan. Likewise, Industrial and Commercial Bank of China's acquisition of a 20 percent stake in Standard Bank of South Africa will provide a platform to support other Chinese companies looking to expand in southern Africa.

Another important rationale for acquisitions will be to secure stable supplies of commodities. Ownership or minority shareholdings of resource companies will provide both a source of profit when commodity prices recover and better ways of securing materials than buying them in spot markets. Such investments also prepare the way for future cooperation, increasing the familiarity and strengthening the relationships of different stakeholders and market participants, and bringing information and insight into the dynamics of strategically important markets. Already the global oil industry is familiar with China's largest players, Sinopec, PetroChina, and CNOOC; a host of other companies are following in their wake. ChemChina, a state-owned chemicals company, spent some $1.4 billion in 2006 buying a series of overseas companies that could supply it with materials; it is now looking for more strategic investments to strengthen its specialty chemicals and life-sciences arms. Minmetals, another state-controlled company, spent just under $1.4 billion to buy a large part of Australia's Oz Minerals in 2009. And other companies are looking for similar deals.

Activity in mature markets will be less visible, but it will occur, especially for Chinese businesses with strong cash positions. Huawei continues to look for ways to establish itself in the United States, in March 2009 agreeing to a partnership with T-Mobile USA for the distribution of Huawei's 3G data cards. Haier is also planning to increase its sales forces in Japan, to allow it to take advantage of the economic downturn to boost sales by 30 percent within a year by pushing its range of inexpensive products.

To make acquisitions work, in both emerging and mature markets, Chinese companies have a great deal to learn. Today, they rely primarily on "hard" power, as political scientist Joseph Nye calls it: they get what they want through sheer financial muscle, scale, and relative strength. But Chinese companies often lack "soft" power: the ability to influence through diplomacy and the raising of mutual interests. This is evident in the failure of several high-profile acquisition bids, such as CNOOC's attempt to buy Unocal in 2005 and Chinalco's bid for Rio Tinto in 2009. For successful acquisitions, Chinese companies, and the officials who support them, need to develop the capabilities to attract, inspire, and persuade all the different stakeholders that are involved. This means not just at the companies being targeted, but in governments where official approval is needed and in the media, so arguments and voices supporting a deal can be heard.

Moreover, postmerger integration problems have beset some of those companies that went ahead. Chinese companies are still learning to manage the process of an acquisition effectively, from retaining customers and key staff to navigating a foreign and usually unfamiliar regulatory and social environment. Li Rongrong, the head of the state-owned Assets Supervision and Administration Commission, the body that holds and manages the government's stakes in the country's largest state-owned enterprises, has long argued that most Chinese companies do not understand the legal risks of foreign acquisitions. Nonetheless, these skills are learnable, and Chinese companies may develop the capabilities of sustaining an acquisition more rapidly than many observers expect.

China As a Game Changer

China's power, as we have seen, stems from the combination of scale and intensity. When that power is moved onto the world stage, the global impact will be immense. Consequently, in an ever-increasing number of industries, China will be a game changer; its presence will fundamentally shift the prevailing business models and basis of competition within those industries.

Only a few companies, such as Huawei and ZTE in the telecommunications equipment-making sector, have demonstrated this potential so far. But more are coming. In the passenger car sector, some independent car firms are proving themselves far quicker at penetrating the domestic market and moving into overseas markets than the massive government-backed companies and their joint ventures with foreign carmakers. Chery Automobile, which was set up in 1997, took less than a decade to make itself China's third-bestselling carmaker. By the end of 2007, it was also the country's leading car exporter, selling 120,000 of its vehicles overseas.

Chery's cars, and those of its rival, Geely, compete almost entirely on price. Chery's bestselling model, the QQ, can be bought for less than $4,500. Geely's cheapest car costs a little less. GM's Chevrolet Spark costs one-third more, and Volkswagen's cheapest model costs nearly double (though it has started to bring car models from its low-cost Czech-based subsidiary, Skoda, to its Shanghai factory, intending to recapture some of the market share it has lost).

Offering goods at a lower price is only one tactic. As I discussed in chapter 3 with the examination of the *shan zhai* or "bandit" practices used by many new businesses, Chinese companies know that they cannot establish themselves on the same ground as existing multinationals, so they have to change the nature of the game. The best way they have found of doing this is to find and produce goods that cause large-scale market disruption.

In its mobile-phone handset business, Huawei took an apparent weakness—its lack of a recognized consumer brand name—to do exactly that. The division's largest deal to date was a five-year agreement to supply 3G phones to the telecommunications services company Vodafone. These phones would only have Vodafone's logo, not the Huawei name alongside it. This made it an unpalatable deal for other leading mobile handset makers such as Nokia, Sony Ericsson, or Samsung, as it undermined their strategy of charging a premium for branded products. But it allowed Huawei to change the business model, and it gave the Chinese company an opportunity to gain experience working with Vodafone, giving it a better understanding of how international companies operate.

Another example of a disruptive strategy is creating new consumers where previously there were none. Both Chery and Geely have concentrated on being able to get cars to market extremely fast. Such lower-tier markets are natural targets for Chery and Geely's inexpensive models. Similarly, BYD, the battery and automobile company, minimizes costs with a semiautomatic manufacturing system featuring low fixed investment and high labor content that takes advantage of China's low staff costs. In addition, it has developed a unique backward-vertical integration model by streamlining its production line and developing key high-cost parts (including chassis, air conditioning, and engine) in-house.

Since BYD began manufacturing cars it has invested heavily in R&D, focusing in particular on car battery and dual gasoline-electric drivetrain systems. If its efforts in these areas prove successful, BYD will have created a key platform to be a leader in the potentially hugely lucrative electric-auto market. If this happens, it could turn out to be one of the most disruptive of all Chinese companies worldwide.

It is also worth noting that China has the largest known reserves of rare earth metals, which are a key ingredient in "new energy" vehicles such as hybrid and electric cars. This represents a competitive advantage for Chinese companies and may be a deciding factor in changing the game for the global automotive industry.

Beyond cars, what about aircraft? This would seem a big leap for a developing nation's economy. But it is official government policy to develop large passenger aircraft and eventually compete with Boeing and Airbus. Given its record over the last couple of decades of establishing a presence in industries previously deemed too technologically advanced for developing countries, it seems clear that this could well be successful. It could also happen within a few years—far less time than the two decades it took Airbus to launch its first commercial aircraft after the French, British, and German governments formally agreed in 1967 to launch the project.

Chinese manufacturers are entering this market in the same way they develop their presence in every industry. First they make components, then sell them at low prices to claim market share; then they acquire competitors. This gives them access to further know-how and expertise, allowing them to move up the value chain and claim areas beyond that of the initial component they made, eventually allowing them to reach a point where entire products can be made.

In 2007, Airbus sourced $60-million worth of components from China; by 2015, it expects that value to have risen to $400 million.[7] In the city of Tianjin, the company's A320 aircraft are being assembled, with the first one completed in June 2009. A separate runway has been built at the city's airport specifically to handle test flights for the aircraft.

Of course, this industry could have a natural advantage with the burgeoning Chinese airline industry, particularly if the market for air travel within China expands. Currently, the industry is expected to need 3,000 passenger and freight aircraft in the two decades up to 2025, with an estimated value of just under $290 billion.[8] Like automobile and telecommunications companies before them, aircraft makers will discover that they cannot avoid building production facilities in China because of the combination of lower costs and better access to China's markets. The challenge for these companies will be to get the balance right: to position themselves for maximum gain while minimizing risk.

Vigilant Leaders

To cope with the magnitude of the challenges China poses, multinational companies need to develop a style of leadership that will succeed over time in these fast-paced settings. In their work on vigilant leaders, George Day and Paul Schoemaker, two professors at the University of Pennsylvania's Wharton School, identify three key traits of such people, all of which are highly relevant for doing business in China:

- *Long time horizons.* A vigilant leader's time horizon encompasses a decade or more. An operational leader is focused on the short term. The vigilant leader's job is to take the company to a new stage in its history; the core task of operational figures is to improve performance at the current stage. Vigilant leaders employ their imagination to probe for potential second-order effects and long-range trends.
- *External focus.* Vigilant leaders are open to new ideas, seek diverse perspectives, listen to a wide array of sources, and foster broad social and professional networks. Operational leaders are more narrowly focused, have less interest in outside opinions, and confine their networking to familiar settings.
- *Organizational skills.* Vigilant leaders enable their people to make decisions and create slack to explore areas outside their main

focus. Operational leaders are more controlling, focus on efficiency and cost cutting, and don't explore outside potential.

In China, companies have to be able to trade off the conflicts involved in the activities of vigilant leaders. They need decisions made fast, without constantly having to seek permission from above or, worse still, from headquarters outside the country. But such decisions have to be made within the framework of a long time horizon; short-term mistakes can be tolerated, provided they also serve other functions, such as testing new ideas or adding to the company's experience and knowledge base.

Chinese companies need operational managers to improve the efficiency of their businesses, especially in the face of China's ever more competitive environment, but they also need vigilant leaders: executives willing to look outside the company or beyond its normal remit of operations to discover ideas and opportunities that could potentially transform the scale or scope of their business and take it to a new height.

The very best Chinese business executives are good examples of vigilant leaders. I have mentioned many of them in this book, and others are becoming more familiar to the public as their companies gain prominence. They include Lenovo's Liu Chuanzhi; Haier's Zhang Ruimin; Hengan's Xu Lianjie; Dongxiang's Chen Yihong; Li Ning's Li Ning and Zhang Zhiyong; BYD's Wang Chuanfu; and Mindray's Xu Hang. Before long, some of these individuals, and other Chinese executives as well, will stand among the recognized models of global business leadership.

EPILOGUE

The Chinese Renaissance

Businesspeople entering China would do well to take the truly long view: a view spanning several centuries. For this country stands on the threshold of a renaissance, one that could see it regain the glory of its greatest era, the Tang dynasty, which lasted from the seventh to the tenth centuries, both China's most open era in history and the greatest period of Chinese influence.

This new resurgence is already beginning to spill from its current economic resurgence to other spheres, especially in science. It is providing examples of innovation and development that everyone can both contribute to and learn from. Living at such a time is a privilege. Participating in the events that are shaping it is even more so.

But whereas during the Tang dynasty (and throughout most of its history) China viewed itself at the world's center—as the "Middle Kingdom"—its new incarnation is far more open. Chinese people see themselves not as dominant, but as participants in the world as a whole. This perception drives many Chinese people, and many Chinese companies, forward. As I have mentioned, some of its best companies have a sense of purpose that extends far beyond simply making money for their owners. Yes, they want to be profitable, world-class companies, but even more so they want to be successful Chinese companies. They want to make a mark on the world at large, and they also want the world at large to make a mark on them.

It is only by having a knowledge of this aspect of China's context that multinational companies can grasp the multifaceted agendas of Chinese companies—what motivates them and why they behave as they do. Possessed with such understanding of China, any company can not simply improve its prospects of success, but also participate in one of the great projects of the twenty-first century.

Through this book we have seen how China, starting from its adoption of openness and market freedoms, has paved the way for multinational companies to migrate ever more parts of their value chains to China. We have seen how the world's best manufacturers are starting to integrate production in China with their manufacturing and marketing operations in the rest of the world, and vice versa.

We have seen how this is opening up possibilities for one world companies and the kind of strategies businesses should be developing to realize these possibilities. A major consequence of this is that China will be shaping our world. At a time of global financial crisis, when many countries are looking inward, China is still looking outward.

China's growth rate may have dropped slightly during the current worldwide recession, as trade and overseas investment retreated. But as the world economy recovers, both companies and countries will be in even greater need of the advantages China and its involvement in the globalization project offers: the efficiencies provided by worldwide supply chains, the net benefits of international trade. Manufacturers will continue to want to produce their goods where costs are lower; information will flow even more freely through the Internet; capital will continue to move around the world in search of a higher return; and China's markets will be an even greater attraction for companies looking to sell more of their products. At the same time, China will become more globally oriented in its search for resources, for markets, for expertise, and for understanding.

For multinational companies, having a China strategy will be essential. The framework proposed by this book for conceptualizing China—its move toward ever greater market liberalization in more and more sectors and the integration of its economy into the global economy—will continue to hold true for the foreseeable future.

Of course, the ideas and conceptual frameworks I have described cannot guarantee success. Given China's complexities, its rate of change, and the infinite number of variables involved that would be impossible. But this book does offer a way to both see what is happening and be able to put this into the context, first, of China and, second, of the world. With this understanding, companies—either those already established in China or those venturing in for the first time—should be better prepared both to anticipate change and to handle unanticipated change. As I noted in chapter 6, instead of focusing just on the "three Cs" in conventional strategy—customers, competitors, and their own company—corporate leaders need to consider a fourth "C": the context.

Successful one world companies will be those that, although excited by the prospects China offers to developing globally integrated businesses, always bear in mind the demands and constraints imposed by local customs at one extreme and the government's agenda at the other. They know that China will remain a place intensely local in its demands on operations. Its markets are a complex mosaic of fragmented elements, divided by geography, culture, income, education, skills, and other factors, further complicated by the rate of change they are all undergoing.

As a good friend of mine, Heather Ting, the chief financial officer of BP's global petrochemicals business, once said to me: "The desire to create a new, better China is always there." Ever present in China is the feeling of having to develop and catch up so that it can be perceived as a nation at the forefront of culture and commerce. This aspiration should not be underestimated; it is a goal that underlies the country's drive and gives many Chinese a motive for realizing success beyond money or power.

The Chinese are patient about this aspiration. But they also realize that many targets that sound rhetorical are likely to be real; maybe not today, but at some point in the future, and possibly sooner rather than later. For business the implications of this attitude are as follows:

- Do not underestimate how much change China can get through in an extremely short time. China has been brilliant at targeting what it wants and then getting it. This does not mean that things will be different overnight, but certainly within the space of just a few years, issues that looked extremely difficult can be moved along surprisingly fast.

- Plan for a better future. Chinese are very optimistic, or at least hopeful, that their country is changing for the better; it would be foolish to bet against them. The country still faces many problems, from environmental degradation to income disparity to corruption. Its people know that many of these problems are systemic and hard to change quickly. But they also compare their country's condition to the way it was before the period of economic reform. They know that China has come a very long way in a very short time. Most Chinese people are justifiably proud of this progress and feel they have reason to hope that other difficult issues will be addressed over time. The how and when may not be clear to them, but for most of them the direction is certain.

- What works today may not work in the future, or even in the very near term. We have seen how surges in demand for different types of goods have been sparked by combinations of regulatory change and consumers surpassing their income thresholds. Such changes can also be negative and are likely to occur as the government strengthens its regulatory regimes. Stricter enforcement of laws is more likely to affect Chinese companies that have been exploiting lax practices in areas such as the environment than multinational companies that have brought in developed-country practices. But other rule changes can hurt international busi-

nesses more than local ones, such as the various attempts by officials to mandate Chinese-developed standards instead of international ones.

- Very little works out fully as planned, so be prepared for changes.
As powerful as it is, official China's writ over industry and the
economy is not complete. Even in core industries dominated by
state-owned companies, developments often turn out other than
as officially designed. Take the auto industry, where China has
gone from nowhere to being the world's number-two vehicle producer (expected to be number one by the end of 2009). Government direction of the industry has helped, but at the same time,
the sector's structure is very different from that envisaged in the
mid-1990s. Instead of being built around three massive state auto
enterprises picked by the government, a series of second-tier auto
companies, nimble and aggressive, have emerged looking more
like potential long-term winners than their giant big brothers.[1]

No other country resembles China. No other country has so many
opportunities—and challenges. And no other time has been so crucial
for entering China as now. The paradoxical truth, however, is that a
China strategy is not a strategy for entering China. It is a strategy for
creating a global business, in a way that prepares for something that
may be happening for the first time in history: the knitting together
of worldwide enterprise into a coherent whole.

NOTES

Chapter 1

1. Li Ning himself is now the Chairman of Li Ning Company. Day-to-day operations are run by its CEO, Zhang Zhiyong.

2. "China Auto Sales Hit 1.14m Units in August," *China Daily*, September 10, 2007, http://www.chinadaily.com.cn/bizchina/2009-09/08/content_8668545.htm; and "China's Top 500 Perform Better Than U.S.," *China Daily*, September 9, 2007, http://www.chinadaily.com.cn/china/2009-09/07/content_8660388.htm (both accessed September 10, 2009).

3. Angus Maddison, *Contours of the World Economy, 1–2030 AD* (Oxford: Oxford University Press, 2007), 340.

4. According to the U.S. Department of the Treasury; see http://www.treas.gov/tic/mfh.txt (accessed July 21, 2009). In 2000, China held barely $70 billion, according to the Brookings Institution; see "Sky's the Limit? National and Global Implications of China's Reserve Accumulation." Available at http://www.brookings.edu/articles/2009/0721_chinas_reserve_prasad.aspx (accessed July 21, 2009).

5. For data on China's GDP and trade performance in 2008, see "Statistical Communiqué of the People's Republic of China on the 2008 National Economic and Social Development," February 26, 2009, http://www.stats.gov.cn/english/newsandcomingevents/+20090226_402540784.htm (accessed October 20, 2009).

6. Shanghai Maglev Transportation Development Co. Ltd. See http://www.smtdc.com/en/gycf3.asp (accessed September 3, 2009).

7. Andrew Cainey, Suvojoy Segupta, and Steven Veldhoen, "The Asian Recovery" (working title), to be published in *strategy+business*, Winter 2009.

8. *China Daily*, op. cit.

9. Zachary Karabelli, "They're Winning: Why Is China's Stimulus Working So Much Better Than Ours?" *The New Republic*, August 1, 2009.

10. Source: China's Ministry of Commerce. See "Experts: China's Outbound Investment Unlikely to Outstrip FDI," *Xinhua News Agency*, July 2, 2009. Available at http://news.xinhuanet.com/english/2009–07/02/content_11667032.htm (accessed July 21, 2009).

11. Pankaj Ghemawat, *Redefining Global Strategy* (Cambridge: Harvard Business School Press, 2007).

Chapter 2

1. China's retail sales: National Bureau of Statistics; *China Economic Quarterly* 13, no. 1, March 2009, 2. U.S. retail sales: U.S. Census Bureau, http://www.census.gov/mrts/www/mrts.html (accessed April 15, 2009).

2. *China Statistical Yearbook 2008* (Beijing: China Statistics Press, 2008), 636. Hereafter referred to as *CSY*; all editions cited were published in Beijing in the year of their title by China Statistics Press, with the exception of the 1998 edition cited in note 8.

3. Ibid., 223.

4. Yang Jian, "Toyota's Underperformance Underscores the Toughness of the China Market," *Automotive News China*, July 15, 2009.

5. According to official accounts, 28.18 million state-owned enterprise workers were laid off between 1993 and 2003, but this is almost certainly an undercount of the true total. See Barry Naughton, *The Chinese Economy: Transitions and Growth* (Cambridge: Massachusetts Institute of Technology Press, 2007), 185–189.

6. *CSY 2001*, 107; *CSY 2008*, 109. Derived by adding total employees for private enterprises and self-employed individuals.

7. *CSY 2008*, 729; Ministry of Commerce announcement, January 15, 2009.

8. *CSY 1998*, 619, 636; *CSY 2008*, 726, 728; General Administration of Customs of the People's Republic of China, 2008, China export. See: http://www.customs.gov.cn/publish/portal0/tab1/info156574.htm.

9. Gerald Adolph and Justin Pettit. *Merge Ahead: Mastering the Five Enduring Trends of Artful M&A* (New York: McGraw-Hill, 2009), 36.

10. Regional GDP figures are derived from *CSY 2008*, 49. See also "Yangtze River Delta, Pearl River Delta and Bohai Rim Cities Lead the Economic Running" (in Chinese) at http://www.gov.cn/jrzg/2008–11/27/content_1161209.htm (accessed April 15, 2009).

11. *CSY 2006*, 99.

12. See Deepak Bhattasali, "The State of the Chinese Economy—A Development Economist's Perspective," World Bank, 2001. Available at http://www.worldbank.org.cn/Chinese/content/chineseeconomy.pdf (accessed April 15, 2009).

13. *CSY 2006*, 389.

14. *CSY 2008*, 606; Length of Transportation route, Chinainfobank, from China Statistics Press 2009.

15. According to Sam Su, in a personal interview conducted in 2008. Also see Warren Liu, *KFC in China: Secret Recipe for Success* (New York: Wiley, 2008).

Chapter 3

1. *China Economic Quarterly*, June 2008, 38.

2. See http://money.cnn.com/magazines/fortune/global500/2009/countries/China.html.

3. By 2005, total utilized foreign direct investment had reached $570 billion, according to the Ministry of Commerce (see "Total Foreign Investment in Actual Use Tops $570 Bln in China," *People's Daily*, March 15, 2005. Available at http://english.peopledaily.com.cn/200503/15/eng20050315_176936.html (accessed May 21, 2009). Another $280 billion was invested between 2006 and 2008. The total for 2009 was forecast at around $80 billion at the time of writing. See *China Economic Quarterly 13*, no. 3, September 2009, 2.

4. Ming Zeng and Peter J. Williamson, *Dragons at Your Door: How Chinese Cost Innovation Is Disrupting Global Competition* (Boston: Harvard Business School Press, 2007), 46–49.

Chapter 4

1. David Shambaugh, *China's Communist Party: Atrophy and Adaptation* (Washington/Berkeley: Woodrow Wilson Center Press/University of California Press, 2008).

2. Melinda Liu, "Right Brain," *Newsweek* Web exclusive, September 8, 2009, http://www.newsweek.com/id/214993 (accessed September 16, 2009).

3. The Pew Global Attitudes Project, "The 2008 Pew Global Attitudes Survey in China," issued July 22, 2008. Available at http://pewglobal.org/reports/pdf/261.pdf (accessed March 6, 2009).

4. Barry Naughton, *The Chinese Economy: Transitions and Growth* (Cambridge: MIT Press, 2007), 464.

5. Melinda Liu, "A Lean, Green Detroit," *Newsweek,* May 4, 2008, http://www.slideshare.net/wrusso1011/newsweek-china-takes-the-lead-in-the-automotive-industry (accessed September 16, 2009).

6. See http://www.hsbc.com.cn/1/2/misc/branches-and-atms.

Chapter 5

1. Samuel J. Palmisano, "The Globally Integrated Enterprise," *Foreign Affairs,* May/June 2006, 127–136. Available at http://www.ibm.com/ibm/governmental programs/samforeignaffairs.pdf (accessed March 4, 2009).

2. Robert Malone, "IBM Moves Global Procurement to China," Forbes.com, October 13, 2006. Available at http://www.forbes.com/business/2006/10/13/ibm-procure-shenzhen-biz-logistics-cx_rm_1013ibm.html (accessed September 15, 2009).

3. Ibid.

4. Thomas Friedman, *The World Is Flat: A Brief History of the Twenty-First Century* (New York: Farrar, Strauss and Giroux, 2005); Kenichi Ohmae, *The Borderless World: Power and Strategy in the Interlinked Economy* (New York: Harper & Row, 1991).

5. "China's Internet Users Exceed 300 Million," Wuhan newspaper (Chinese language), July 17, 2009, http://news.sina.com.cn/o/2009-07-17/103215969496s.shtml (accessed September 15, 2009).

6. Martin Wolf, "Wheel of Fortune Turns as China Outdoes West," *Financial Times,* September 13, 2009.

7. Noam Scheiber, "Peking Over Our Shoulder," *New Republic,* September 15, 2009.

8. Associated Press, "China Showcases Commercial Jet at Asia Air Show," September 8, 2009; Polly Huin, "China Unveils Jet at Asia's Biggest Air Show," Agence-France Press, September 8, 2009.

9. For a full list of Chinese companies in the Fortune Global 500, see http://money.cnn.com/magazines/fortune/global500/2009/countries/China.html (accessed September 14, 2009).

10. 2008 OFDI, Minstry of Commerce of the People's of Republic of China, Department of Outward Investment and Economic Cooperation, February 19, 2009. Available at http://fec.mofcom.gov.cn/tjzl/jwtz/215102.shtml; *2007 Statistical Bulletin of China's Outward Foreign Direct Investment.*

11. See Arthur Kroeber and G. A. Donovan, "Sudan Oil: Where Does It Go?" *China Economic Quarterly* 11, no. 2, Q2 2007, 18.

12. David Barboza and Michael Wines, "Mining Giant Scraps China Deal: Rio Tinto Ends Plan to Sell $19.5 Billion Stake to Chinalco," *New York Times,* June 4, 2009. Available at http://www.nytimes.com/2009/06/05/business/global/05mine.html (accessed September 15, 2009).

13. David Barboza, "News Media Run by China Look Abroad for Growth," *New York Times,* January 14, 2009. Available at http://www.nytimes.com/2009/01/15/business/worldbusiness/15tele.html (accessed April 5, 2009).

Chapter 6

1. Booz Allen Hamilton (now Booz & Company) and the American Chamber of Commerce in Shanghai (AmCham), *China Manufacturing Competitiveness 2007–2008,* 2008, AmCham; and Booz & Company and AmCham, *China*

Manufacturing Competitiveness 2008–2009, 2009, AmCham. The study surveyed sixty-six manufacturers belonging to AmCham's Manufacturing Business Council.

2. See Geoff Dyer, "China's Wary Shoppers Set Store by Western Brands," *Financial Times,* September 4, 2007. Carrefour's controversial methods of fueling its growth have been widely documented. For one example, see Shu-Ching Jean Chen, "Carrefour Contends with Bribery in China," August 27, 2007. Available at http://www.forbes.com/markets/2007/08/27/carrefour-bribery-china-markets-equity-cx_jc_0827markets03.html (accessed September 15, 2009).

3. The rise of D'Long is entertainingly told in "The Great Consolidator," *China Economic Quarterly,* Q1 2004. For details of what happened to Tang Wanxin, see "Tycoon Jailed in China's Largest Stock Scandal," *Shanghai Daily,* May 1, 2006. Available at http://www.chinadaily.com.cn/china/2006–05/01/content_581687.htm (accessed June 18, 2009). Kelon was subsequently acquired by another leading Chinese maker of white goods, Hisense; see "Hisense to Take over Kelon for US$85 Mln," Xinhua News Agency. April 24, 2006. Available at http://english.china.com/zh_cn/business/appliances/11025897/20060424/13271449.html (accessed June 18, 2009). Ningbo Bird's rise and fall is briefly documented in "Is Ningbo Bird's Goose Cooked?" United Press International, July 19, 2005. Available at http://www.physorg.com/news5293.html (accessed June 18, 2009).

4. AmCham, *2008 Business Report,* AmCham, 2009.

5. Joe Studwell, "Dream, Dream, Dream . . . ," *China Economic Quarterly,* Q4 2004, 24.

6. For details of Volkswagen's turnaround strategy for China, see http://www.volkswagen-media-services.com/medias_publish/ms/content/en/pressemitteilungen/2005/10/17/volkswagen_group_presents.standard.gidoeffentlichkeit.html (accessed December 11, 2007).

7. Adapted from Ronald Haddock and Christoph Bliss, "Integrating China into Your Global Supply Chain," Booz & Company, February 2008, 4–5.

Chapter 7

1. James Pomfret and Joanne Chiu, "BYD Aims to Sell 700,000 Vehicles in 2010," Reuters, July 2009. Available at: http://www.reuters.com/article/company News/idUKHKG36676120090727 (accessed September 19, 2009).

2. The company's rise is examined in an article by Ronald Haddock and John Jullens, "The Best Years of the Auto Industry Are Still to Come," published in *strategy+business,* no. 55, Summer 2009. An account of production innovations at its battery business can be found in Peter J. Williamson and Ming Zeng,

"Value-for-Money Strategies for Recessionary Times," *Harvard Business Review*, March 2009, 66–74. See also Norihiko Shirouzu, "Technology Levels Playing Field in Race to Market Electric Car," *Wall Street Journal*, January 12, 2009.

3. "Yum! Takes Bite of China's Little Sheep," March 2009, What's on Xiamen.com. Available at http://www.whatsonxiamen.com/wine_msg.php?titleid=495.

4. See http://szb.qzwb.com/dnzb/html/2009-04/14/content_31314.htm.

5. See http://www.fdimagazine.com/news/fullstory.php/aid/1146/China_claws_back_the_tax.html.

6. See http://research.nokia.com/node/252.

7. Nandani Lynton and Kirsten Høgh Thøgersen, "How China Transforms an Executive's Mind," *Organizational Dynamics 35*, no. 2, 2006, 170–181.

Chapter 8

1. Geoff Dyer and Jamil Anderlini, "Man in the News: Huang Guangyu," *Financial Times*, November 28, 2008. Rick Carew and Jackie Cheung, "Three Private-Equity Firms Vying for Stake in Chinese Retailer GOME," *Wall Street Journal*, May 28, 2009; Wong Ka-chun, Tim LeeMaster, and Jasmine Wang, "Bain in HK$3.6B Deal to Acquire GOME Stake," *South China Morning Post*, June 13, 2009, Yu Ning and Wang Shanshan, "Gome Hatches Plan to Raise HK$3 Billion," *Caijing Magazine*, June 16. 2009.

2. Joseph S. Nye, "Soft Power, Hard Power and Leadership," October 2006. Available at http://www.hks.harvard.edu/netgov/files/talks/docs/11_06_06_seminar_Nye_HP_SP_Leadership.pdf (accessed December 30, 2008).

3. The Pew Global Attitudes Project, *The Chinese Celebrate Their Roaring Economy, as They Struggle with Its Costs: Near Universal Optimism about Beijing Olympics,* 2008, Pew Research Center, Washington, DC, 14–15.

4. Economic Observer Online staff, "China's Stimulus Package: A Breakdown of Spending," *Economic Observer Online,* March 7, 2009, http://www.eeo.com.cn/ens/finance_investment/2009/03/07/131626.shtml (accessed September 20, 2009).

5. Booz & Company and AmCham Shanghai, "China Manufacturing Competitiveness 2008–2009."

6. Kirby Chien, "China Sourcing Safe, but with Caveat," Reuters, September 7, 2007. Available at http://www.reuters.com/article/TheChinaCentury07/id USPEK17996020070907 (accessed December 4, 2007).

7. According to Airbus; "More Than 3,000 Aircraft Needed on the Chinese Mainland in Next 20 Years," Airbus press release, February 14, 2007. Available at http://www.airbus.com/en/presscentre/pressreleases/pressreleases_items/07_02_14_Chinese_Mainland_EN.html (accessed December 13, 2007).

8. George Day and Paul Schoemaker, "Vigilant vs. Operational Leaders: Changes at Ford, the Coke-Pepsi Fiasco, and Other Management Moments," September 20, 2006, Knowledge@Wharton, http://knowledge.wharton.upenn .edu/article.cfm?articleid=1553 (accessed September 19, 2009).

Chapter 9

1. Christian Koehler and Ronald Haddock, "China's Auto Policy: Structured for Success?" *Auto Focus Asia*, no. 1, 2007, 16–20.

ACKNOWLEDGMENTS

This book would not have been possible if not for the collective effort and wisdom of a group of exceptional individuals. Their time, advice, expertise, and support have enriched the book's materials and have helped immensely in pulling together a series of observations through the years into a coherent and cogent piece of work.

I wish to thank our partners at Basic Books. Tim Sullivan deserves particular gratitude for his vision and early belief in the book's appeal to the broader market and how this book can help others navigate for success in the China market. His role with this book was much more than that of publisher, and we are better for it. As project editor and copy editor, respectively, Laura Esterman and Gray Cutler raised the quality of the material and—equally importantly—kept it moving so that it would be both timely and relevant.

The China Strategy draws deeply on the experience of corporate leaders I know, who have both inspired me with their insights and demonstrated how critical it really is to have a novel, integrated approach when dealing with China. I am grateful to many people, among them the following individuals who specifically contributed to this book: Michael Cannon-Brookes, Paul Etchells, Warren Liu, Josef Mueller, Sam Su, Shane Tedjarati, Heather Ting, Wang Jialin, Wang Zhihong, and Zeng Ming.

Many colleagues at Booz & Company contributed significantly. I learned a great deal about globalization and the role of China in it from working on numerous client engagements with my fellow partners. A special thanks to Ron Haddock, who has helped shape many of the theories and frameworks in the book. I would also like to thank Shumeet Banerji, our firm's CEO, for his encouragement on this project, along with Andrew Cainey and Bill Russo, for their insights and knowledge as well as time in reviewing the manuscript.

I also would like to acknowledge the effort and insight brought by a number of other staff members who worked on this project, both directly and indirectly. This includes Bill Bai, Yu Huang, Steven Jiang, Xia Jin, Tao Ke, Yichin Lee, Elizabeth Liang, Kevin Ma, Chris McNally, Ben Mok, Sarah Ng, Fushing Pang, Arnold Sun, Edwin Tong, Adeline Wong, Alex Wong, Guang Yang, Raymond Yeung, Kenny Yip, Ting Zhao, Jessica Zhang, Tina Zhang, and others who, while they are not specifically named here, made much-appreciated contributions.

Thanks to our team of professionals devoted to intellectual capital and marketing at Booz & Company. They helped make this book a reality. Those involved directly with this book include Jonathan Gage, Richard Sanderson, and Ella Mak. I would also like to thank Jim Levine, our literary agent, for his frank comments and guidance through the process. A special thanks goes to Linda Eckstein, who created all the diagrams and tables for the book, for her creative touch.

A special acknowledgment and thank you is owed to Grace Leung. Grace was the guiding force behind the project, helping to articulate the book's value, organizing the process, making sure that all the pieces were in place, and holding the project steady through its entirety.

It is difficult to articulate the nature of the contribution that our firm's editor-in-chief, Art Kleiner, provided. His perseverance and dedication to the quality of the idea, and his firm grasp on how to integrate the many rounds of feedback and comments—coming from a very diverse group—are unmatched, and I am deeply thankful. Without Art, this would not be the same book. I am also thankful to the firm's chief marketing and knowledge officer, Tom Stewart, who helped us navigate the marketing environment.

ACKNOWLEDGMENTS

I owe a huge debt of gratitude to Simon Cartledge, who as consulting editor helped with all the major elements of the book, from developing the initial draft through to the final end product. This book benefited from his knowledge of the business environment in China and his tireless effort and patience through our many rounds of changes and refinements into making this book what it is now.

I would also like to take this opportunity to thank Bob Ching for introducing me to consulting in China all those years ago and for serving as a long-time mentor.

To others who deserve credit, but whose names were inadvertently left out from this list—thank you.

Finally of course, I am most grateful to my family, Grace, Karen, and Kevin; they provide ongoing inspiration and support for me—and, in doing so, help me to achieve my personal best in delivering the essential advantage to all our clients.

INDEX

For more information about the ideas in this book, see
www.thechinastrategy.com